SEX & DRUGS
& **sport** & **cheating**

A brief history of sport and cheating

SEX & DRUGS
& sport & cheating

A brief history of sport and cheating

Paul Anthony

First published 2014 by DB Publishing, an imprint of JMD Media Ltd, Nottingham, United Kingdom.

ISBN 9781780914169

Printed and bound by Copytech (UK) Limited, Peterborough.

Contents

This work is dedicated to all those who try to make sport an honest and honourable endeavour

1. The Greatest Show on Earth

According to George Orwell, sport is war minus the shooting. Nations can do battle without the bloodshed and destruction. It brings honour. It needs courage and sacrifice. At the highest level it requires great dedication. In war it is essential to win at all costs, but even war has rules. The Geneva Convention dates back to 1864 and in Europe the Code of Chivalry was accepted throughout the Middle Ages. The Duke of Wellington claimed that the Battle of Waterloo was won on the playing fields of Eton. He was an Old Etonian. In sport we are told that it is not the winning that counts but how we play the game. Not everyone believes this and many have used nefarious means to win acclaim. In other words they cheated. Some things are not actually illegal but they may be thoroughly bad sportsmanship and most of us would strongly disapprove. Sport is entertainment and it is big business, capable of turning sportsmen into millionaires. At the highest level the concept of the amateur sportsman is effectively dead. There is prize money. There is sponsorship and there is the potential to earn money from advertising and endorsement.

The ancient Olympic Games is generally regarded as the oldest athletic or sporting competition in the world. It started in 776BC. Originally there was just one event, a sprint of about 200 metres. Other events were added over the years including some longer races and there was usually a military orientation. The old martial events are with us today in the javelin and discus competitions. The sprint remained the first and most prestigious event. The winner of an event was awarded an olive wreath and had a red ribbon tied around his head or possibly an arm or leg. Medals are a modern innovation but in the ancient games only the winner received an accolade. There was a strong military orientation in the Games and in war coming second is not good enough. There was great emphasis on the worship of Zeus, the Greek king of the gods and in AD393 the Roman Emperor Theodosius I who was a convert to Christianity banned the games.

The competitors were naked and only men participated. It is often believed that women were barred from watching the games, but this is not entirely true. Married women were forbidden under penalty of death. Perhaps this was in case they became dissatisfied with what they had at home. Two contrasting groups of women who were permitted at the games were prostitutes and virgins. Prostitutes would have seen it all before whilst virgins were probably window shopping. Not only the women were potentially titillated by the handsome physiques and rippling muscles, the Ancient Greek army was renowned for its acceptance if not encouragement of homosexuality. They seemed to think that they would fight more fiercely if they had a special relationship with the man next to them.

There is just one recorded occasion of a married woman, or at least a widow being caught at the games. She was a daughter of the head of a family of successful athletes. Disguised as a trainer she brought her son to the games after the death of her husband. The son won the boxing contest and in her joy she jumped over the fence which separated the trainers from the athletes. She caught her clothes on the fence and they came off leaving her standing naked in the ring and in no position to deny her attributes. However, out of respect for her father, brothers and son who were all Olympic champions, she was not punished. Perhaps other women were successful in attending in disguise, rather like the women at the stoning in Monty Python's *Life of Brian*.

Although women could not compete, they could still win an event, as in the chariot races the winner was the owner of the horses rather than the driver. There were games for women called the Heraean Games, after the goddess Hera who was the wife of Zeus. This may date back as far as the men's games or perhaps only to the 6th century BC. Spartan women were dominant. Exercise was important in their culture whilst

Greek women rarely took any. The women were not naked but wore a short dress. This mini-dress was a little off the shoulder number and off one breast too. In competition this skimpy dress with nothing under it would leave very little to the imagination. Nevertheless, the Heraean Games are much less documented than the full frontal nudity of the men's Olympics. Like the Olympics, it was held once every four years.

There were also Games, for boys and from the 3rd century BC there were three categories. There were no weight categories but age was used to delineate them. However, proof of date of birth would have been difficult as this was well before birth certificates. Most were in the Pythian Games or the Isthmian Games, although there was another group called ageneioi. The exact age groups are uncertain but one authority suggests that Pythian boys were between 12 and 14 years, Isthmian boys were 14 to 17 and ageneioi were between 17 and 20 years old.

The Pythian Games were held at Delphi in a sanctuary called Pytho. According to the legend this was where the god Apollo killed the dragon Python. The Apollo sanctuary dates to the 10th century BC and became world famous for the Oracle of Delphi where the future was supposed to be foretold. Many rulers in the region would consult the oracle to help them to make decisions.

The Isthmian Games were held on the Isthmus of Corinth and dedicated to the god Poseidon who was god of the sea but also patron of chariot races. In the first century AD there were also Isthmian Games for girls.

The ageneioi does not refer to any god or place but in Greek it means "the beardless ones". They would be teenagers who had not yet developed significant facial hair. The age categories were probably based not so much on years as on physical maturity.

Any free man from the Pan-Hellenic region could compete. This was a wide geographical area from Sicily to the Black Sea. Non-Greeks and slaves were excluded.

THE MODERN GAMES

The Olympic ideal did not die in AD393 but lay dormant to re-awake in the unlikely place of mid-19th century England. Dr William Penny Brookes (1809–1895) was a local doctor in Wenlock in Shropshire. He was both a practicing doctor and a magistrate. He was very interested in public health and tackled local sanitation and hygiene. His own classical schooling inspired him to revive a modern Olympic fellowship to promote a "moral, physical and intellectual" movement. Thus the modern Olympics has its roots in an English public school. He held the first Olympiad in Wenlock in 1850. He was an ardent campaigner for the Greek establishment to hold a revived Olympic Games. Eventually the philanthropist Evangelis Zappas (1800–1865) financed a new Athenian Olympic Games in 1859 and William Brookes donated a stipend for the prize money. However, it would be many years before professional athletes would be allowed to take part in the Olympics and even now those who participate receive honour but not money.

In 1861 he introduced the Shropshire Olympic Games and in 1865 he set up a National Olympian Association (NOA) which was based in Liverpool. This evolved into the modern Olympic Movement. The following year he was involved with the first British National Olympic Games at Crystal Palace in London. He repeated these games and publicly proposed an international Olympic event in the Greek press in 1881. He was keen on sport as a means of promoting health and fitness for the public at large. That vision is with us today and widely embraced by those who promote public health. It was part of the long term aim or legacy of the London Olympics.

In 1886 the winner of the 400 yards hurdles at the games was a W.G. Grace. He also played football for a London club called The Wanderers which was composed mostly of former public schoolboys. Of course he was most renowned for cricket, which took so much of his time that he did not qualify as a doctor until he was 31 years old. The inimitable W.G. Grace will be mentioned again. He may have been an impressive all-rounder at sport but he was not very sporting.

In 1890 Dr William Brookes received a visit from the celebrated French educator Baron Pierre Frédy de Coubertin (1863–1937), who is credited as the founder of the modern Olympics. The baron was impressed by the Olympiad and organised an international Olympic congress at the Sorbonne in Paris in 1894. Baron de Coubertin made Dr Brookes an honorary member of the congress, but he was unable to attend because of illness. The congress led to the creation of the International Olympic Committee and then the first modern Olympic Games which were held in Athens in 1896. Unfortunately William Brookes died in 1895 and so he never saw his dream become reality.

The motto of the new Olympic movement was *Citius, Altius, Fortius* which is Latin for *Faster, Higher, Stronger*. That motto remains. It suggests that the aim is purely the furtherance of human achievement rather than the more altruistic aspects of sport. As we shall see, perhaps that is a true reflection of the Olympic ideal. Dr Brookes may have preferred *mens sana in corpore sano* meaning *a healthy mind in a healthy body* or *it is not the winning that counts but the taking part.*

In 1904, alongside the Games there was a fair which offered its own sporting events. These included Anthropology Days in which a group of "savages" recruited from the fair's international villages competed in a variety of events. They included a greased-pole climb, ethnic dancing and mudslinging. In the 21st century we are quite appalled at such grotesquely racist spectacles but more than 100 years ago people thought differently. One person who was not amused was Baron Pierre de Coubertin who noted, "As for that outrageous charade, it will of course lose its appeal when black men, red men and yellow men learn to run, jump and throw, and leave the white men behind them." Nowadays runners of African descent dominate every race from the sprints to the marathon. The baron had vision.

The Olympic Games has taken place every four years since its inauguration in 1896 except for 1916, 1940 and 1944 when world wars made this impossible. The Winter Olympics was introduced in 1924 and was initially held in leap years along with the Summer Games but from 1994 they were held on the even number years between leap years. There were Winter Games in 1992, 1994 and 1998. The Games are planned well in advance and the 1916 Games should have been in Germany. Both Summer and Winter Games should have been in Japan in 1940 and in 1944 the Summer and Winter Games should have been in the UK and Italy respectively. Needless to say, this was impossible in all three years.

The origin of the marathon race is well known but perhaps not the details that surround it. The Persians, who were the dominant military force in the region landed at Marathon, about 25 miles from Athens in 490BC. The Athenians sent a runner to Sparta to request their help in the imminent battle and he covered the 150 miles in just two days. However, there was no time to wait for the Spartan army. The Persians greatly outnumbered the Athenians by perhaps 4:1 as well as having an awesome record in battle. Perhaps this led the Persians to arrogance and overconfidence. The Greeks were fighting for survival of their city and their state. Contrary to the usual format of battle, the Athenian army did not walk towards the Persian ranks but ran at them, taking the battle to the enemy. Despite being heavily outnumbered by a battle-hardened army they won a historic victory. The body count was said to be 6,400 Persians to 196 Athenians. A runner was sent to Athens to tell its citizens. He delivered his message and then fell down dead. He would have been exhausted and dehydrated from the battle before he set out for Athens and he may also have lost blood. The marathon was never part of the Ancient Games but the run was honoured by a race of 40 kilometres from the advent of the Modern Games. In 1908 when the Games was held in London the race was lengthened slightly to 26 miles, to run from Windsor Castle to the White City stadium. A further 385 yards was added so that the race could finish in front of King Edward VII's royal box. After much heated debate 26.2 miles was established as the official marathon distance at the 1924 Olympics in Paris.

When the modern Olympics started in 1896 women were excluded but in 1924 a significant number of events for women were introduced. In athletics women now do all the long distance events that were formerly the preserve of men. They also do the pole vault and throwing the hammer. The projectiles for shot, javelin, discus and hammer are lighter for women. Men do a decathlon of ten events whilst women have a heptathlon of seven events, with shorter distances to run. Women now do most of the same events as men, including boxing and weightlifting.

The 2012 London Olympics saw for the first time both male and female competitors from all competing nations including even two token women from Saudi Arabia. Many conservative clerics in Saudi Arabia were opposed to this and women's sport there is very limited. In response the International Olympic Committee (IOC) was considering banning Saudi Arabia if they prevented women from competing. Sarah Attar competed in the 800 metres in athletics and Wodjan Ali Seraj Abdulrahim Shahrkhani competed in the judo competition. The latter caused a problem when she was expected to wear a hijab, the traditional Muslim headdress as the World Judo Federation thought that it was unsafe in a fight. The 16-year-old heavyweight was allowed to wear a briefer form of headdress which still covered her hair. Women do not take part in Greco-Roman style wrestling although they compete in freestyle wrestling. The former was under threat of being dropped from the Olympics partly because of the absence of female participants but also because it does not seem so attractive to television viewers. It first became an Olympic sport in 706BC. However, shortly after announcing that Tokyo will host the 2020 Games the IOC also announced that Greco-Roman style wrestling will be reinstated. Synchronised swimming is a sport for women only at the Olympics and this does not please some British male synchronised swimmers. It seems that men only sports may be barred but women only sports are permitted. Beach volleyball does have both male and female teams but it is the women who attract the crowds, at least crowds of men. It is not so much their athletic prowess as being "well fit" in street parlance that grabs the attention. The only events in which men and women compete in the same competition on equal terms are the equestrian events as the muscular work is done by the horse.

PARALYMPICS

The first para-Olympic Games were held in Stoke Mandeville in 1948, the year of the post-war Austerity Games in London. Four years later competitors from Holland joined the Games and what is now known as the Paralympic Movement, was born. Olympic-type Disability Games were held in Rome in 1960. In 1976 in Toronto extra groups of disabilities were added and in the same year the first Paralympic Winter Games took place in Sweden. The term "Paralympic Games" was adopted in 1984 by the International Olympic Committee.

Stoke Mandeville Hospital in Buckinghamshire was, and still is the National Centre for Spinal Injuries. The development of care for those with spinal injuries was dramatized in the BBC programme "*The Best of Men*" in 2012. At the beginning of the Second World War men with spinal injuries were brought to Stoke Mandeville in boxes that bore a sinister resemblance to coffins. They were not removed from those boxes but lay on their back heavily sedated with morphine. They were denied such basic nursing care as frequent turning to prevent pressure sores. The attitude seemed to be that there was no point in taking them out of their coffins as they would soon be back in them again. They were just kept quiet to die. Mortality was 80% within a year of injury and those who did survive were hidden away in long-term institutions for "incurables". In 1944, with the risk of more spinal injuries as a second front was opened, the British Government asked Dr Ludwig Guttmann to run the spinal injuries centre. He was a German Jew who had fled from the Nazis. His ideas met with considerable opposition, partly because he was a German Jew but largely because they were so revolutionary. Patients were left lying on their backs because if they were sat up their blood pressure would drop and they would faint. He found that if they were gradually introduced to an upright position the blood vessels would accommodate and they could comfortably sit up in bed or in a chair. He introduced good nursing care and removed the excessive sedation. The result was a rather noisy, obstreperous ward and this spawned more criticism. However, what it represented was young men getting their fight and vitality back. He encouraged a competitive streak and encouraged sport from wheelchairs. It is fascinating to see the old, heavy chairs of 1948 and to compare them with modern racing chairs. Ludwig Guttmann retired in 1966 and was knighted for his remarkable achievements.

The trouble with the Paralympics is that there are so many different types of disability and hence so many categories. As well as spinal injuries there are those with amputations but they vary in the site and number of amputations as well as the level. Categories include blind or partially sighted and mental handicap. Some have congenital abnormalities. The swimmer Ellie Simmonds has achrondroplasia which is a hereditary form of dwarfism with a normal size body but short arms and legs. Very good efforts have been made to get some standardisation but it must always be incomplete.

In 2012 Oscar Pistorius of South Africa became the first person to compete in both the normal Olympics and Paralympics when he raced in the 400 metres. There was some controversy about whether his carbon fibre blades gave him an unfair advantage compared with those who run on their own legs, but he failed to reach the finals. However, in 1904, before there were Paralympics, George Eyser won three gold and three other medals in the gymnastics despite having a wooden leg.

The ancient Olympics started as just one event but it grew to be a number of events including boxing, wrestling and chariot racing. So too the modern Olympics has grown in size and scope. A new record was set in the Summer Games of 2012 when 205 nations competed in 300 events in London. The Russians also boast a record for a Winter Olympics with 85 counties competing in 98 events, bringing 6,000 athletes to Sochi in 2014. The International Olympic Committee (IOC) would like a cap on the size of the games with a limit of about 10,500 competitors. The ever increasing numbers make organisation and logistics very difficult and an ever increasing size of the games will make it prohibitively expensive to host.

The Olympic Games has become *The Greatest Show on Earth*. It is watched by billions of people around the world. They look for sport at its best and they certainly get performance at its best. Whether the rest lives up to the expectation of sport we shall see.

2. Cheating in the Ancient Olympics

Because the ancient Games were so long ago most contemporary manuscripts have been lost and this is a great impediment to knowing exactly what happened. However, the Greeks were keen to record the misdeeds that occurred and we do have records carved in stone. They refer only to the more gross cases of misconduct. They prove that the urge to win is great and for some the temptation to do so regardless of the means is irresistible. Competition would have been robust and interpretation of the rules probably liberal. They would have regarded us as soft with our modern approach. Therefore what they would count as cheating would have to be quite blatant and anything less was acceptable. In events such as chariot racing serious injury and death at times were inevitable. There were 12 judges called Hellanodikai and they were considered to be honest by and large, but there were exceptions. The historian Plutarch suggested that umpires, called brabeutai sometimes awarded crowns incorrectly. Whether this represented incompetence, corruption or merely a difference of opinion between Plutarch and the brabeutai is unclear. Perhaps Plutarch was like a modern football fan who always knows far better than the referee. Competitors who were found cheating could be punished by flogging. However, a stiff fine was more usual. If the athlete could not pay the fine his city would pay instead. On the way to the stadium there were a number of bronze statues of Zeus. They were called zanes and their erection was funded by the fines imposed on those who were caught. On the plinths of the statues the offenders were named and their offence recorded for posterity. This is how we know about them.

Most of the offences relate to bribing opponents. A number of athletes changed their allegiance from one city state to another and whilst this did not seem to offend the founders of the Games the abandoned city states took great exception to it. National pride was as strong as ever.

Fouls within a competition such as low blows, biting, or tripping opponents during a race were punished by a sharp blow with a rod called a rhabdos. As the athletes were naked this would have had a sobering effect.

Athletes received lectures on the greatness and fairness of the Games during their compulsory training before the Games. Competitors swore an oath that in nothing would they sin against the Olympic Games. If they believed that the gods in whose honour the Games were held were looking right down on them it should have dissuaded them from cheating. However, fame and glory is enticing. So too is prize money.

Astylus of Croton won the stade and diaulos races in 488BC. The stade is the original sprint race of about 200 metres. It was still regarded as the premium race of the Games. Stade became a unit of distance and it gives us the modern word "stadium". The diaulos was about 400 metres and was a two stade race. In 484BC Gelo, tyrant of Syracuse convinced him to race for his city instead of Croton. In those days tyrant was an acceptable job description rather than a term of abuse. The people of Croton assumed that Astylus had been bribed and they tore down his statue and seized his house.

Olympia was a shrine rather than a city and both Pisa (not to be confused with the one in Italy) and Elis claimed control. The Eleans sought to make the Olympic Games a positive experience for all concerned. A truce called the *ekecheiria* was enforced for one month during the Games but this was later extended to three months. During the truce athletes and presumably trainers and spectators from the belligerent city states could pass through enemy territory in peace and safety. In 420BC the Eleans fined the Spartans 200,000 drachmai for attacking Fort Phyrcus and for sending heavy infantry into Lepreum during the truce. They had such power. The Spartans refuted the charge and refused to pay the fine. Consequently the Spartans were banned from participating in and offering sacrifices at the games that year.

However, a Spartan named Lichas entered his own chariot team under the pretence of being Thebans. He gave the game away by choosing to tie the winning ribbon on his chariot himself. The Hellanodikai had him flogged as punishment.

In 388 BC a boxer named Eupolus was found to have bribed all three of his opponents to let him win. The Hellanodikai fined all four of them and the fines paid for a row of bronze statues of Zeus with inscriptions explaining their crimes. These six bronze statues were the first of the zanes.

In the 100th Olympics, Sotades of Crete who had won the long distance race for Crete the previous time, competed for the city of Ephesus. The city of Crete sentenced him to banishment.

In 332BC Callipus of Athens bribed his fellow competitors in the pentathlon. They were discovered and the Hellanodikai fined them all. Athens sent an orator to convince the authorities to revoke the fine but he was unsuccessful. The Athenians refused to pay and withdrew from the Olympics. It took an intervention from the Oracle of Delphi to persuade Athens to pay and a second group of six bronze zanes were erected from the fines.

Two more zanes appeared in 68BC after Eudelus paid a wrestler from Rhodes to let him win a preliminary wrestling competition. The city or Rhodes paid the fine. In AD125 two Egyptian boxers were convicted of fixing a match and two further zanes were built.

On one occasion a citizen of Elis called Damonikos had bribed the father of his son's opponent. Both fathers were fined.

The Alexandrian boxer Apollonios arrived late at Olympia because he had fought in a local event with high prize-money. Competitors were expected to arrive about a month before the start of the Games for the official preparation period. He was also found to have lied about this to the hellanodikai. He funded another zane.

The Alexandrian Sarapion was fined for withdrawing from the pankration when he was called for a contest. This was seen as cowardly. Pankration means "all force" and it is a very free style of martial art with a combination of wrestling and boxing. Everything was permitted except biting, gouging the opponent's eyes, nose or mouth and attacking the genitals. During the preparation period an athlete could withdraw if he felt that he had no chance of winning and it was seen as more honourable to withdraw than to face defeat. However, once the Games commenced withdrawal was not permitted. Again this is based on the art of war, that it is better to avoid a battle than to lose. The Pankration was regarded as the ultimate skill in the martial arts and the prize money was the greatest of all the sports except for the equestrian events. However, serious injury was less likely in the Pankreation than in boxing. Boxing did not have rounds and the fighters battled until one submitted. They wore rather hard leather gloves and injuries were common.

Sometimes, especially in the martial arts, a competitor was so dominant that all his opponents would withdraw during the preparatory stage and he would win by default. Such a victory was called "akoniti" which means "without dust" as the victor did not have to enter the dusty fighting ring. Such a victory in running races was exceptionally rare.

The Romans and Ancient Egyptians both tried to expunge the memory of people who were despised and erase them from history. The Romans used the term *damnatio memoriae* from which we get the word damnation. The Egyptians erased their names from monuments. The Greeks on the other hand set up memorials and inscriptions so that their misdeeds would not be forgotten or forgiven. The cheats became immortalised but not the way they wished.

We may think that drug abuse is a form of cheating that is limited to the present day. Certainly people tried it in the past and it was not then illegal. The famous Greek physician Galen described how athletes would be given various concoctions of herbs to improve their performance. Perhaps this is rather like some of the supplements so ubiquitous amongst modern athletes. Greek athletes also ate sheep's testicles. This may be the first attempt to use anabolic steroids but this was unlikely to have had much effect.

The Ancient Olympics lasted for over 1,000 years and there were 16 zanes to commemorate those who were caught cheating. We know about them from the captions on the plinths. The modern Olympics has been going for around 120 years, but if we had zanes to commemorate the cheats who have been caught there would be many more than that. It is generally assumed that cheating in the Ancient Olympics was rare but in both old and new it is important to remember that we only know about those who have been caught. How many how have cheated and not been caught is purely speculation.

3. Gender Bending

A ny primary school teacher will confirm that in the very early years there is little difference between the physical abilities of boys and girls but within a few years, and certainly well before puberty, boys become faster and stronger. Hence males and females compete in separate events while the Ancient Greeks had separate games. Women's sport has come a long way in recent years but performance still lags behind men's sport, even in long distance running events where power is not as important as stamina. We may see gender verification simply as preventing a man from competing in women's sport but the reality is much more complex. Certain masculine features give an unfair advantage in women's sport and gender assignation is not as simple as may be presumed.

Stanisława Walasiewicz was born in Poland in 1911 and her family emigrated to the United States when she was two years old but they did not take American citizenship. They changed her name to the anglicised Stella Walsh when she started school. She ran for Poland in the 1930s and was a major force in women's sprinting in the 1930s. She was the first woman to run the 100 yards in less than 11 seconds with a time of 10.8 seconds in 1930. She set world records for the 100 yards, 100 metres, 220 yards and the long jump. She had an unusually long career lasting from 1930 to 1954 during which she set 20 world records and won 41 American national titles although she did not take American citizenship until 1947. She won the gold medal for the 100 metres in the 1932 Olympics but only managed silver in 1936. She was so incensed at being beaten by the American Helen Stephens that she complained to the authorities that to have run that fast her opponent must be a man. This claim will prove to be ironic. The German authorities investigated and found that

Helen Stephens was indeed a woman. A picture of the medal ceremony shows her towering over Stella Walsh. She was a very tall and muscular woman who also won the events of throwing the discus and putting the shot. She was said to be unbeaten in her entire athletics career.

Stella Walsh was a very shy person who would arrive at an event in her kit and she would leave as soon as the race was over. She never changed or showered with the other competitors.

In December 1980, at the age of 69, she was loading her car in a shopping area when she was caught in the crossfire of an attempted armed robbery. She was hit by a stray bullet and was killed. She was taken to the mortuary and many accounts say that she was stripped and found to be a man. However, it was more complex than that. According to the coroner's report she had a condition known as mosaicism. This is where there is a mixture of chromosomes in the body and she was said that have more male than female cells. Some say that she had both ovaries and testes. It would seem that her parents thought that she was a girl but her genitalia were probably ambiguous and this is why she avoided exposing them to others. She never married.

In the 1936 Olympics Dora Ratjen replaced Gretel Bergmann who had been expected to win a gold medal for Germany in the high jump. Gretel Bergmann was politically incorrect for Germany in 1936 as she was Jewish. Dora Ratjen managed only fourth in the women's high jump in the 1936 Olympics but she beat the world record in the European Championships in Vienna in 1938. On the way back to Cologne after the event she was stopped by a policeman at a railway station and accused of being a man despite having the identity card of a woman. Dora was examined by a doctor who confirmed that this was a man. A criminal investigation followed but charges were dropped. In January 1939 Dora's father wrote to the registry officer, requesting a change of sex and change of name to Heinrich on all official documents.

She was later disqualified from medals and records for being a man although this was really another intersex case rather than an obvious man masquerading as a woman. There was said to be uncertainty at birth. She was brought up as a girl but by about 11 years old she felt that she was really a boy. However, she was unable to discuss this with her parents. When interviewed many years later she, or by then he, claimed to have been forced into the charade by the Nazis "for the honour and glory and Germany" although there is evidence that the Nazis knew nothing of the deceit. Having previously minted a stamp in her honour they were highly embarrassed by the revelation.

The problem is ambiguity of physical features but the male characteristics can give an advantage with a stronger body. In 1946 the International Amateur Athletics Federation (IAAF) introduced a rule that female competitors must bring a medical certificate to prove that they are eligible to compete. This gave no uniformity of criteria or assurance of honesty. There were often allegations that some of the beefy women from the Soviet Bloc who competed in the power events must be male and in 1966 the IAAF decreed that all female athletes should undergo gender verification. At this point the Ukrainian sisters Irina and Tamar Press dropped out of competition. Basically the early tests involved being examined by a panel of three female doctors. For years the concept of a "sex test" for female athletes gave ample fodder for cartoonists. Many athletes felt that it was embarrassing and demeaning. In 1976 Princess Anne represented Great Britain and as the daughter of the Queen she was exempt although this would have been irrelevant as she was competing in an equestrian event.

The simple physical examination does not easily differentiate the intersex conditions. No one strolled into the examination with meat and two veg swinging in the breeze. The athletes hated it and it was replaced by chromosome analysis. Human cells contain 46 chromosomes in 23 pairs. There are 22 pairs called autosomes, one of each pair from each parent and a pair of sex chromosomes that determine gender. The sex chromosomes, also one from each parent, are called X and Y as under the microscope they look rather like the letters. A person with two X chromosomes is female. A person with an X and a Y is male. The Y chromosome is what leads to male development. The X chromosome contains rather more genetic material than the Y and often one of the X chromosomes in the cell is inactive. This can be seen on a stained cell and is called a Barr body after Dr Murray Barr who described it. It was hoped that simply taking a scrape from the inside of the cheek to obtain cells, smearing it on a microscope slide and staining it would offer a reliable test.

It was never very satisfactory and advances in technology called polymerase chain reaction (PCR) techniques allowed Barr body analysis to be replaced with PCR analysis in 1991. This gave a much more reliable picture of the chromosomes.

The trouble is that the situation is nothing like as simple as possession of two X chromosomes or an X and a Y. There are a number of abnormalities of the sex chromosomes. Turner's syndrome is called XO as there is just one X chromosome and no Y or second X chromosome. They look female but are short and infertile with ovaries that are just streaks. There is no athletic advantage. More common, but still fairly rare, is Kleinfelter's syndrome or XXY. There are 47 chromosomes, including two X chromosomes but also a Y. They are often tall but have no athletic advantage and appear male rather than female but with poorly developed genitals. There is also a rare condition with three X chromosomes. Because of this they are sometimes referred to as "super females" although in reality there are far from super. They may be tall and they may be fertile but they usually have learning difficulties.

There is a condition called androgen insensitivity, formerly known as testicular feminization, in which the person has XY chromosomes but the body is unreactive to the Y chromosome and hence appears as a normal female. This person appears female but is infertile and has no athletic advantage over XX women.

Congenital Adrenal Hyperplasia (CAH) is due to an enzyme deficiency, not an abnormality of the sex chromosomes. It affects the enzymes that synthesize the steroids hormones that include the sex hormones. Even at birth it can lead to high androgen levels giving female babies ambiguous genitalia. Hence, if there is error, it will be in assigning a girl as a boy and not the other way round. Treatment with cortisol is required and sometimes surgery. It is not seen as an advantage for athletics.

An abnormality that affects the hormones but is acquired rather than congenital is called polycystic ovary syndrome (PCOS). Typically such women are overweight or obese with hirsutism (male hair distribution), irregular or absent menstruation and low fertility. It may be tempting to believe that low fertility in fat, hairy women is due to a shortage of men willing to get them pregnant. This is wrong. There is apparently no shortage of willing candidates. Not all sufferers are overweight or obese but an important finding is that levels of both oestrogens (female hormones) and androgens (male hormones) are raised. Oestrogens and androgens are not unique to either men or women. Both have both, but oestrogens predominate in women and androgens predominate in men. Therefore, having the condition is rather like taking anabolic steroids but there is no intention to ban such women from competition.

The concept of gender is not as clear as we may think. It involves physical, physiological and psychological issues. It is certainly not a simple matter of XX or XY. If someone who has always thought of herself as being female is told that she is really male, this must be a devastating psychological blow. Mandatory gender testing was officially stopped by the International Olympic Committee in 1999, although there can be evaluation of individual athletes if the question arises.

The first athlete to fail a gender test was another Polish sprinter. Ewa Kłobukowska had won a gold medal in the women's 4x100 metres relay and a bronze medal in the women's 100 metres in 1964. In 1967 she was found to have a rare genetic condition which gave her a mixture of XX and XXY cells in her body. She was banned from competing in Olympic and professional sports.

The Czechoslovakian runner Zdenka Koubkova changed sex from female to male to become Zdenek Koubek in 1936. The British shot putter and javelin thrower Mary Weston became Mark Weston following a series of operations shortly after 1935. In both cases there had been no evidence of physical rather than psychological male attributes before the operation.

Another athlete who changed from female to male was the former East German shot putter Heidi Krieger who is now Andreas Krieger. She was born in 1966 and like many East German athletes was put on a training regime that included liberal doses of anabolic steroids (male hormones). She was said to have changes to her body by the time that she was 18. As will be seen later, male distribution hairiness and a deepening of the voice are common. The latter does not reverse on stopping the drugs and neither does enlargement of the clitoris. The athlete blamed the drugs for the psychological problems and has had a sex change operation. However, as many other East German women were also forced to take anabolic steroids too it is uncertain just how much this did contribute. Andreas Krieger is now married to the former East German swimmer Ute Krause who was also a victim of massive doping by East German sports officials.

Under current IOC rules, transsexuals who have had a sex change from male to female can compete in women's events at the Olympics two years after the operation. Richard Raskin was born male and was the captain of the Yale University Men's Tennis Team. In 1975 he had sex change surgery to become female, changing his name to Renee Richards before trying to compete in the US Open Tournament. After a long, drawn out and much heated court battle, she was allowed to compete in 1977. In 1999, she expressed regrets about her decision to undergo such an operation.

Looking at pictures of Stella Walsh in running kit it is clear that if a man was to try to masquerade as a woman it would be easier with the athletics attire of the 1930s than in modern kit that leaves little room to hide anything. Swimming costumes cover more than they used to but they are tight and hiding the "family jewels" would be very difficult. In addition, drug testing now involves producing a specimen of urine in front of an official of the same gender so that the likes of Stella Walsh and Dora Ratjen with abnormal genitalia would have been unable to hide.

The problem of gender verification will not go away. In 2006 the Indian runner Santhi Soundarajan who had won a silver medal in the Asian games in Qatar, failed the gender verification test and was stripped of her medal. Details were not officially given in the name of medical confidentiality but it is rumoured that she had androgen insensitivity. As noted earlier, this gives no advantage despite the XY chromosomes. However, an 800 metres runner who has caused much greater controversy is Caster Semenya from South Africa. She won the 800 metres at the 2009 World Athletics Championships in Berlin at the age of 18 but her appearance and demeanor attracted much attention. The IAAF confirmed that she had agreed to a testing process that began in South Africa and would continue in Germany. In July 2010, the IAAF confirmed that she was cleared to continue competing as a woman, although the results of the gender testing were never officially released for reasons of privacy.

The South African athlete looks far more muscular and masculine than the Indian who was banned. She has a great deal of facial hair and talks with a deep voice. Furthermore, the posture assumed on winning is hardly feminine and seems instead to be bragging about the enormous muscles. This looks like polycystic ovary syndrome but in the absence of confirmation this is just speculation. Sex chromosomes may be normal but the question of whether this is fair competition with normal female athletes will not go away. Some 800 metres athletes have been banned for taking anabolic steroids. Should high levels of androgens as the result of a disease be acceptable, whilst taking anabolic steroids leads to disqualification and ignominy? Both have the same effect. It seems that individuals who have abnormality of their chromosomes may be disqualified, even if it gives no advantage, whilst those who have an illness that gives them high levels of male hormones and a clear advantage are allowed to compete. It makes no sense.

There have been allegations about basketball player Brittney Griner who is 6ft 8in tall and has a deep voice as well as being openly gay. Most of the allegations seem to be based on intuitive hatred rather than evidence. She turned down the opportunity to represent the USA in the 2012 Olympics basketball team and this has led to further suggestions that she was afraid of a gender verification test. Perhaps she was just afraid of name calling and bullying on an international level. The low voice does suggest a high level of androgens and the hair line does seem a little receded, although this may be due to a style that pulls her hair back rather tightly rather than male pattern baldness. She does not look as facially hairy or as muscular as Caster Semenya. It seems strange that the US basketball authorities (the WNBA) have not asked for a test. Perhaps they are afraid of the outrage from some quarters or perhaps they realise that as the results are not given for reasons of medical confidentiality, that it will not lay the allegations to rest. She may have normal chromosomes but high levels of androgens. However, her great advantage in that sport is her height and those hormones will not have caused that. Basketball is not a contact sport but a large, powerful frame is still an advantage.

In 2013 another gender row blew up in South Korean Women's football. The Seoul City striker Park Eun-Seon was at the centre of the controversy. Coaches from six of the seven WK-League sides threatened a boycott and they also asked the Korea Women's Football Federation (KWFF) to bar Park from playing until her gender is verified. At the age of 26 she said that she had had several gender verification tests from the age of 15. She did it for the World Cup, for the Olympics and for several other events. Each time she has been cleared but still the allegation recurs. Her own club supported her saying that to demand a gender examination is a serious violation of a person's human rights and it insults that person's character. She was not selected for the South Korean team in the 2010 AFC Women's Asian Cup after the host nation China raised questions about gender. It seems that no one dares to upset China. Although the concept of medical confidentiality must remain sacrosanct, perhaps it is time for her to choose to publicise the results of her tests if they are clear and should lay the matter to rest.

I was tempted to say that there had been no case of a male athlete masquerading as a female until I came across a case from 2005. Samukeliso Sithole was an athlete from Zimbabwe who at age 18 had won seven gold medals the previous year. She had been touted as one of the young talents to emerge from the country. The athlete was arrested for being a man who had impersonated a woman for financial gain but the authorities did not know whether to remand to a male or female prison. Six witnesses, including two doctors said that the athlete was a man. The person had claimed to be a hermaphrodite with both male and female sex organs but in court, admitted to being a man. His real name was Fadzai Fuzani. The athlete also claimed to have periods and feared becoming pregnant. I think this should be viewed with great scepticism. Sithole said the male organs became enlarged after a traditional healer took revenge after not being paid for treatment the previous year. The trouble is that in a country such as Zimbabwe it is very difficult to know exactly what is happening. It still seems unclear whether this was truly an overt man after financial gain from prize money or another intersex state, but it may well be the former. A story from 2011 does seem to suggest that this was fraud. Fadzai Fuzani acquired the birth certificate of Samukeliso Sithole with the help of teachers at his school. He still tries to compete in boxing and netball events as a female but his cover has been blown a couple of times.

This does seem to be a genuine case of a man masquerading as a woman in sport. I am reluctant to say that it is unique but it certainly does seem to be a rarity and most cases of controversy have been over ambiguity rather than overt fraud.

Another gender issue is related to fairness rather than competition. The quest for equality in sport led to pressure for women to be awarded the same prize money as men in the Wimbledon Lawn Tennis Championship and the organisers succumbed in 2007. Men play the best of five sets, women the best of three. The quality of the men's game is much greater with longer rallies and the women's game is more often one-sided with shorter sets. They probably spend about half the time on court to reach the finals compared with the men. This means that it is much easier for women to compete in the doubles as well as the singles events. Hence, in the name of equality, women can earn more money than men for playing an inferior game. As the slogan in George Orwell's *Animal Farm* reads, "All animals are equal – but some are more equal than others."

4. Just Plain Cheating

The gender issue is usually a grey area rather than cold, calculated, premeditated cheating, but there are plenty of examples of the latter. Today, when cheating in sport is mentioned people think immediately of performance enhancing substances but we should not forget the old fashioned ways of cheating too.

MARATHONS

In the first of the modern Olympics in 1896 there were 25 athletes registered for the marathon race but only 17 started and a mere nine finished. Of the starters, one was British, one American, one Hungarian and the other 22 were Greek. Spyridon Belokas came in third, just ahead of Gyula Kellner but the latter lodged a complaint that the former had gone round part of the course in a horse and carriage. Investigation confirmed the allegation and he was stripped of his bronze medal.

At the 1904 Olympics in St Louis, Fred Lorz of New York won the marathon in three hours and 13 minutes. Many club runners can do better than that today. He had been exhausted at nine miles but his manager gave him a lift in his car. Technology had now moved from the horse and carriage to the horseless carriage. However, it was 1904, the car broke down and he had to run the rest of the way. He claimed it was a joke but the Amateur Athletic Union were not amused and banned him for life. He was reinstated the following year when he apologized and they found that he had not intended to defraud! He won the Boston Marathon in 1905, presumably on his own two feet.

The nature of the marathon makes it fertile ground for cheating in the traditional sense. Perhaps the most blatant affront and the gold medal for cheating goes to Rosie Ruiz in the 1980 Boston Marathon. She crossed the finishing line in the very impressive time of two hours and 32 minutes, making her the winning woman but the lack of sweat on her clothing or body immediately raised suspicions. She was also unknown. When Bill Rodgers who had just won the male event asked her about her splits, she had no idea what he was talking about. Splits or split times are times for various portions of the race as any serious runner would know. Then two Harvard students claimed to have seen her running out of the spectator section into the race only half a mile from the finish. A photographer remembered meeting her on the subway during the 1979 New York Marathon when she was supposed to be running and she used this time to qualify for the Boston Marathon. Boston Marathon race officials struck her name from the records, and stripped her of her title.

In the 1984 Berlin Marathon a boy of just 16 finished minutes behind the leader. No one believed that such a youngster could have achieved such a time honestly but no one could disprove it either. It would have been interesting to know how he did in future races. By the mid-1990s microchips in shoes were introduced and individuals were monitored every five kilometres. This means that it is possible to measure how long people take over each five kilometres section and when the supposed speed defies belief, or a monitoring point is missed an explanation is sought. In a Berlin Marathon in which more than 30,000 crossed the finish line and everyone lined up for their medals, 127 were questioned about their times over certain sections of the course. The explanations were often imaginative. One runner claimed that he ran barefoot for the first 33 kilometres for health reasons and put on his shoes for just the final seven kilometres. Who said that the Germans do not have a sense of humour?

The Comrades Marathon in South Africa is called an ultramarathon as it is 56 miles from Durban to Pietermaritzburg over arduous terrain. In 1993 a runner from Stellenbosch called Herman Matthee took a taxi for 25 of the 56 miles of the race. He was banned for 10 years. A senior referee of the race believed that he had done the same the previous year too.

Roberto Madrazo was a hopeful candidate for the Mexican Presidential election of 2006 but his Institutional Revolutionary Party had a reputation for election fraud. It seems that whether he ran in elections or marathons he had to cheat. He finished the Berlin Marathon of 2007 in two hours and 41 minutes, winning his age group. However, electronic chips for runners to wear to monitor their pace had been introduced and it revealed that he missed two checkpoints and supposedly ran nine miles in 21 minutes. That is nearly 27mph compared with 22.5mph for 10 seconds in the 100 metres. He was disqualified.

Perhaps politicians just have problems with the truth. Paul Ryan, Republican Party vice presidential candidate to Mitt Romney in the American 2012 elections, claimed to have run a marathon in less than three hours. Some people were so impressed that they researched his claim. He had run one recorded marathon in 1990 and finished in just over four hours. Why could he not just tell the truth? Simply finishing a marathon is most commendable.

China gained another world record in 2010 in the Xiamen marathon in southern China when 30 of the first 100 competitors were disqualified. Most were students who were hoping to earn extra points for their university entrance exams by finishing in less than two hours and 34 minutes. This would be a very impressive time. Some of the runners took cars. Some had other people running for them. Others gave their timing devices to faster runners, some of whom carried at least three chips with them. This was a new world record for the most cheats in one race.

At the 2010 London Marathon, 69-year-old Anthony Gaskell crossed the finishing line at three hours and five minutes, to set a new record for the over 65 age group. Closer analysis showed that he had supposedly run the second half of the race (13.1 miles) in less than an hour. Even a world class runner could not do this. He had missed a loop of the course, skipping miles 13 to 23. He later blamed an injury and said he was trying to get to the finish to receive medical attention. His honorary plaque and title were revoked.

Montreal has bicycle stations throughout the city so that people can rent a bicycle in one location and return it elsewhere. One runner in the middle of the 2011 Montreal Marathon joined the bike-rental scheme to get a qualifying time for the Boston Marathon. He was caught in a photograph and banned from the race for three years.

Rob Sloan of the Sunderland Harriers running team finished third in the 2011 Kielder Marathon in Northumberland. It was a wet and horrible day and at 20 miles he was exhausted and so he boarded a bus to the finish line. He then hid behind a tree before returning to the race. The bus carried spectators to the race and many remembered seeing him on the bus. He confessed and was stripped of his medal and disqualified.

DOUBLE TROUBLE

Still in the realms of marathons, Sergio Motsoeneng and his brother Arnold looked similar and both were distance runners. In 1999 they switched places in the Comrades Marathon at least twice to finish unexpectedly high in ninth place. They were exposed when video revealed that the brothers wore watches on different wrists and the watches apparently changed sides during the race. They were banned from the race for 11 years and did not receive the 6,000 rand (around £370) in prize money. Sergio was allowed to return in 2010 but was disqualified again for testing positive for performance enhancing drugs.

There is a similar story from the London Marathon and it involved two African identical twins. One ran the first half of the race and the other the second half. At the halfway stage they sat down on the kerb together and changed shoes as the trainers contained a chip to monitor them. Everything was well planned except for one detail. They both wore Swatch watches, a popular brand at the time but one had a yellow strap and the other was pink. However, another account gives the two colours as red and green. A sharp observer of the official video recordings noted that the watch strap seemed to change colour halfway through the race and so they were uncovered.

Another case of cheating twins involves cricket rather than marathons. Nazib and Zahid Mohammed are twin brothers from Liverpool. Both are very good at cricket but Nazib is a bowler and Zahib is a batsman. In July 2009 Nazib played for Liverpool and District Cricket Competition's representative side in the President's Trophy against Nottinghamshire Premier League. After bowling, it was Nazib's team's turn to bat but his place was taken by Zahib. What perhaps aroused suspicion was that Nazib had been bowling right handed but Zahib batted left handed. For a person to bowl and bat the other way round is not unheard of but it is very unusual. The pair were discovered and banned from representing that club or playing in that league again in 2009. They did not even prosper as Zahib was out for a duck.

TOOLS OF THE TRADE

Cheating comes in many other guises and many other events. Fencing is one of the five disciplines in the modern pentathlon. In the electric foil, when the weapon touches the opponent an electric circuit is completed and a buzzer sounds to register a score. In the Montreal Olympics in 1976 a Soviet fencer called Boris Onishchenko seemed to be doing rather too well. He was scoring even when he did not appear to have touched his opponent. His British opponent Jim Fox protested vehemently to the officials. The judges agreed and took away the sword to examine it whilst Onischenko was allowed to continue with a replacement. It was found that the epée had hidden wires that allowed the fencer to register a hit by pulling a hidden trigger. He was disqualified and sent home in disgrace.

AGE

In women's gymnastics being young is an advantage because of the flexibility of the adolescent spine, but because of the many problems associated with training children to compete amongst the best in the world competitors have to be over 16 years old for major competitions. The Chinese Women's Gymnastics team narrowly won the team Gold Medal in the Beijing Olympics in 2008. However, all the experts agreed that some of the team were underage. Rumours about the age of three of the team, Jiang Yuyuan, Yang Yilin and He Kexin abounded. The Chinese authorities were adamant that they were all at least 16 years old, but the gold medal winner on the uneven bars, He Kexin had her date of birth recorded as 1 January 1994 on many online records. This made her 14. Her passport, which was issued six months before the Olympics, gave her date of birth as 1 January 1992. This implies official connivance.

Jacques Rogge, president of the International Olympic Committee said it relied on the international federations and it was not the task of the IOC to check such matters for 10,000 athletes. They could have made an exception when there was such an outcry about girls who had not yet reached puberty being said to be 16. They could also make an exception when a national body seems to be failing in its duty. As so often nowadays, everyone seems reluctant to upset the Chinese. The Chinese authorities were complicit in the fraud and this was quite transparent. As one website put it, the silver medallist looked old enough to be the gold medallist's baby-sitter. He Kexin was 1.30 metres tall (4ft 8ins) and weighed 33kg (5st 2lbs). She did not look 16 years old.

In 2010 the Chinese gymnast Dong Fangxiao had her Olympic bronze medal from 2000 rescinded along with several other medals after FIG, the world governing body of gymnastics found that she had falsified her age and competed in 2000 when she was just 14 years old. There was official outrage in China but the ordinary people were angry with their own authorities who let this happen rather than the governing body who found her out. A picture of her at the Olympics shows a little girl. The official story from China was that she or her family must have forged her passport. It is most unlikely, given the Chinese record, that anyone actually believes that.

DISABILITY

In the 2000 Paralympic Games in Sidney the Spanish intellectually-disabled basketball team brought dishonour to a new level. They won gold with an impressive performance but the glory faded when the

Spanish Paralympic Committee discovered that 10 of the 12 members of the team had no mental deficiency. In addition, participants in table tennis, athletics, and swimming events had no disability.

It is amazing that normal people will pretend to be disabled to win the transient glory of an inappropriate medal, but the scale of this deceit is quite astounding. It involved many competitors and must have included coaches and managers too. As we shall see later, managers and officials are not without sin. At least the Spanish Paralympic Committee were honest.

WAYS AND MEANS

Sometimes a person's dreams of glory are constantly thwarted by one person who is always just a little better. There are three ways of defeating your nemesis. The first is to train harder, the second is to train smarter and the third is to get someone to kneecap your opponent.

Nancy Kerrigan and Tonya Harding were both top skaters. On 6 January 1994 they were both at a practice session for the U.S. Figure Skating Championships in Detroit. Jeff Gillooly who was Tonya Harding's ex-husband and her bodyguard Shawn Eckhardt hired Shane Stant to break Nancy Kerrigan's leg so that she could not skate. He failed to find her at her training rink in Massachusetts, so he followed her to Detroit where he struck her on the thigh above the knee with a collapsible police baton. Her leg was only bruised rather than broken but the injury forced her to withdraw from the national championship. Tonya Harding won the event, but both skaters were selected for the 1994 Olympic team. After Tonya Harding admitted helping to cover up the attack the US Figure Skating Association and US Olympic Committee started proceedings to remove her from the Olympic team, but when she threatening legal action they backed down. The American legal system strikes again. She finished eighth in Lillehammer, whilst a fully recovered Nancy Kerrigan won the silver medal.

Jeff Gillooly, Shane Stant, Shawn Eckhardt, and the getaway car driver Derrick Smith were all sent to prison for the attack. Tonya Harding pleaded guilty to conspiracy to hinder prosecution of the attackers with a plea bargain to avoid further prosecution. She received three years' probation, 500 hours of community service and a fine of $160,000. As part of the plea bargain she withdrew from the 1994 World Figure Skating Championships. The US Figure Skating Association conducted an investigation and stripped her of her 1994 US Championships title and banned her for life either as a skater or a coach. They concluded that she knew about the attack before it happened and that she had displayed "a clear disregard for fairness, good sportsmanship and ethical behaviour". That is one way of putting it. They control only the amateur sport and so she tried to turn professional but this failed as no one was prepared to work with her. Few will wonder why. She continued to maintain her innocence and had an angel tattooed on her back, supposedly as a symbol of her innocence.

INEQUALITIES AND INNOVATION

Leaving aside such technical innovations as a button on a fencing sword to register false hits, the quality of equipment can be very important. In the Winter Olympics, skis, sleighs and clothing can be very sophisticated and extremely expensive. The same applies to bicycles and boats, both for rowing and sailing. A large racing yacht is a prohibitive price. As equipment becomes more sophisticated and more expensive we have to ask if sport is for all or is sport just for the elite who can afford it. If all but the wealthy or those with massive sponsorship are effectively excluded from the sport it becomes a battle between expensive technologies rather than between sportsmen. We cannot ignore new technology but perhaps not all should be embraced. Often major innovations are viewed with concern but they may be accepted later. The introduction of the fibreglass pole for vaulting produced a vast surge in performance. Now everyone uses one. Equipment is extremely important in the Paralympics and can be very costly. Blade runners run on high technology and a sports wheelchair can cost £3,000. Perhaps this explains, in part, why there are so few Paralympic athletes from the poorer countries although there are other considerations such as the facilities available for rehabilitation and the status accorded to disabled people. Some countries regard handicap as an embarrassment to be hidden away. In Britain we felt that way until the second half of the 20th century. Hitler would probably have had them all exterminated.

Plimsolls with rubber soles were possible after the vulcanisation of rubber by Charles Goodyear in 1837 but in 1890 a British company called J.W. Foster and Sons developed spikes. The company is now called Reebok. However, the first spikes may go back to 1852. In 1925 a German called Adi Dassler took the technology a stage further. It takes little imagination to deduce that the firm is now called Adidas. As far as I can see, the authorities in athletics did not object to this innovation. Starting blocks may have been viewed with relief as before that, runners would use a trowel to dig a hole for their feet and this would damage the cinder track.

In the 1960 Olympics in Rome the gold medal in the marathon was won by an Ethiopian called Abebe Bikila. He was unknown and a replacement for an injured teammate. He had no sophisticated training. He ran barefoot and yet he broke the world record to win the race. This was exceptional. Zola Budd ran barefoot for South Africa in the 1980s but she took to shoes to protect herself from other competitors' spikes as much as anything. Now that sprint races and swimming races are timed to one hundredth of a second, just the slightest advantage may mean the difference between first and fourth place, between a gold medal and none. No one can ignore technology.

Swimmers shave their bodies as they believe that the drag from hairy arms and legs may slow them down. This led to the development of a suit from neck to wrists and ankles to reduce drag through the water. Each suit costs hundreds of pounds and may need replacement after just three or four races. Some even give added buoyancy. FINA, the governing body of world swimming, banned these suits in 2010. Only textile suits with relatively minimal coverage are allowed.

Cycling had a similar problem in 1993 with aerodynamic bicycles and some that had the riders almost lying down to reduce wind resistance rather than in the traditional upright position.

By 1984 some men were throwing javelins more than 100 metres and there was a danger that they would throw beyond the throwing area and hit someone. The javelin was redesigned to put its centre of gravity in front of its centre of pressure, so that its nose pitched downwards in flight. This reduced distances by about 10%. However, javelin manufacturers were able to increase distance by increasing the javelin's tail drag by roughening the tail surface with holes or dimples. This pulled the centre of pressure back toward the centre of gravity and improved flight. Nowadays, in an international javelin competition a selection of sanctioned javelins is available for competitors to choose, but personal javelins are banned. In 1991 javelin tail roughening was banned and all records achieved with such javelins were nullified. Distances have crept up again but not yet reached 100 metres.

Sometimes the issue is technique rather than technology. Look at how the style of the high jump has changed from the days of the scissors and then the western roll to today. When Roger Bannister become the first man to break the four minutes barrier for the mile in 1954 he used pacemakers who dropped out exhausted as he went along. There were some grandees, including Harold Abrahams who was portrayed in *Chariots of Fire*, who felt that this was unsporting. What is acceptable and what is not has changed so much over the years.

MONEY

A matter that has changed beyond recognition is the question of amateur status. From the beginning of the 20th century until well into its second half, amateur and professional competitors were kept well apart. The amateur status could so easily be lost by taking payment. Even having a job in a sports centre or as a PE teacher may classify a person as a professional. Harold Abrahams courted displeasure by employing Sam Mussabini who was a professional coach. He wanted the best. In *Chariots of Fire* the character of Lord Andrew Livsey, played by Nigel

Havers is fictional but the image of him practicing the hurdles with a glass of champagne perched on the edge of each shows that sport was often a pastime for the very rich.

Jim Thorp won gold medals in the 1912 Olympics in the pentathlon and decathlon. However, he was rumoured to have played American football, baseball and basketball for money. This was probably true. He lost his Olympic titles after he was found to have been paid for playing semi-professional baseball for two seasons before competing in the Olympics. In 1983, some 30 years after he died, the International Olympic Committee (IOC) restored all his Olympic medals.

Paavo Nurmi, known as the flying Finn as he was such a fast distance runner was banned from the 1932 Olympics as it was claimed that he had received too much money for his travel expenses to a meet in Germany. This was instigated by a Swedish official and the people of Finland were so incensed that Finland refused to participate in the traditional athletics tournament between Finland and Sweden until 1939.

By the 1960s and 1970s the supposed position of athletics as an amateur sport was a masquerade. There are stories of organizers asking the officials to leave the room before the appearance money and prize money was distributed to the athletes. It was such a farce that it had to change.

The cold war saw many sham amateurs, often called "shamateurs" for whom being amateur was a thinly veiled illusion. In the Soviet Union and Eastern Europe they were in the armed forces, but they spent most of their time training for their event with the best coaches and facilities that the state could provide. The USA had and still has many generous sports scholarships to its universities. The academic requirements to earn such a scholarship are not generally onerous but great sporting prowess is essential. The academic demands on the individual are also variable and the length of the degree course is rather elastic. What is invariable is the excellent quality of the coaching and training facilities that are offered. In the UK the only university sporting event to get massive national coverage is the Oxford and Cambridge boat race, but college sport in the USA often vies with professional sport for the public's attention. It brings in a large amount of money to the colleges and so recruiting the best is taken seriously. There are rules about direct payments to students that are clearly broken as well as ways round the rules to give benefit in kind. The top scholarship athletes are said to get the best accommodation on campus, their choice of course, their textbooks for free and they do not pay for their kit. Carl Lewis was the recipient of such a scholarship. Ben Johnson was brought up in Canada but still would have been eligible except that his academic prowess was below even the modest standard expected for a sports scholarship.

Some sports became rather more lax rather earlier than others in terms of amateur status. In the 1970s a judo champion was in trouble with the British Judo Association for having been in an advertisement for Mars Bars in which he was shown training for judo. Athletics at club level is still governed by the Amateur Athletics Association (AAA) in England, but UK Athletics governs the elite performers who are far from amateur. The trouble is that being a world class competitor is not something that can be achieved whilst holding down a day job. Sponsorship is required to enable athletes to train and perhaps to have expensive equipment, the best coaches and the best facilities as well as to attend international competition. It was in 1982 that the International Association of Athletics Federations (IAAF) first sanctioned the idea of athletes being paid. Before then brown envelopes, cash under the table and grossly inflated expenses were common. David Jenkins, the 400 metres runner, recalls submitting an expenses claim for £3 that was received by an official who immediately added two more zeros. International athletics meetings are now often called a *grand prix* which means big prize. Top class athletics is a well-paid sport. Even the Olympics accepted professionals after 1988. It includes the highly paid professional tennis players, Premier League football players and the extremely well paid NBA stars from American basketball amongst its competitors. They are not just professionals. They are sporting millionaires.

In contrast, the post-war London Olympics of 1948 were called the Austerity Games. Times were hard throughout the world after years of world war and there were no generous sponsors to shoulder the cost. The athletes even had to bring their own sandwiches for lunch.

It is often said that Hitler snubbed Jesse Owens by refusing to present him with any of his four gold medals at the Munich Olympics in 1936 but it is also argued that he was not actually scheduled to present any of those medals. Some suggest that it was not Hitler who gave Jesse Owens his greatest snub but the American people. However, this might not be entirely fair. He did receive a "ticker-tape parade" on his return to the USA, an honour that was not granted to Carl Lewis when he repeated the feat of four gold medals in 1984, but Jesse Owens did not reap fame and fortune afterwards. Perhaps this was a sign of the times. If anyone can name a white athlete who did half as well but who earned fame and fortune from the 1936 Olympics it would make a case, but amateur status then was strict. In his teens Carl Lewis met Jesse Owens when the latter was working in a dry cleaner's shop. Carl Lewis is said to have declared at an early stage in his career that he wanted to be a millionaire and he never wanted to have a normal job. He was certainly one of the best paid "under the table" athletes at the time. Athletes were supposed to receive no more than $7,200 from their trust fund for expenses but both he and Ben Johnson lived in large houses and drove fancy cars with a lifestyle that did not reflect a frugal standard of living. They were supposed to be getting "cost of living" expenses from their sports authorities. What is cost of living depends upon what you expect from life.

ILLEGAL OR IMMORAL

Sometimes the problem is not overt foul play but very bad sportsmanship yet the authorities can still take action. The badminton doubles of the London 2012 Games saw farcical displays in which pairs of players that were already through to the next round sought to lose the match to gain a more favourable draw. It was one of the few occasions when the crowd booed as top class players put serve after serve into the net. Two pairs of players from South Korea and one pair each from China and Indonesia were disqualified for not trying to win. There was also controversy about not trying on the athletics track. Taoufik Makhloufi of Algeria ran the fastest time in the 1,500 metres heats and was well placed to win a medal. The following day he was in the 800 metres heats as he had not been withdrawn to let him concentrate on the 1,500 metres. As the race started he moved off slowly, jogging behind the other competitors until at about 150 to 200 metres he left the track and abandoned the race. The IAAF decided his performance was against the spirit of the Games and contrary to rule 142.2 which allows expulsion for "failure to compete honestly with bona fide effort". He immediately saw a doctor, complained about an injury to his knee and received a medical certificate. The IAAF reinstated him, he ran the 1500 metres the next day without a hint of injury and he won the gold medal. Comparing his performance in the 800 metres with the 1500 metres the day before and the day after, this appears to be a gross abuse of medical certification and both the athlete and the doctor should be investigated.

There is nothing new about thoroughly bad sportsmanship, even in the quintessentially fair game of cricket. W.G. Grace was averse to being given out and on one occasion when an umpire raised a finger to indicate his dismissal he is reputed to have said, "They have come to see me bat, not you umpire." He refused to walk. On another occasion the Essex fast bowler Charles Kortwright was frustrated at the repeated refusal of the umpire to give Grace out. Eventually he knocked two stumps clean out of the ground. As Grace walked past him on his way back to the pavilion he said, "Surely you're not going doctor? There's still one stump standing." Even when tossing a coin to see who bats first, Grace would call "The lady" which could mean either the Queen's head on one side or Britannia on the other.

No examination of this subject of immorality rather than illegality would be complete without looking at the "mind games" that are so often part of modern sport. This is on public display at its worst as boxers meet for the weigh-in before professional fights. Perhaps their brains have been hit so often that subtlety is not their strong point or perhaps it is just a pantomime for the crowd. Basically the idea is to say something that will distract the opponent and so concern him that he does not concentrate fully on the task in hand. The most adept at this was Mohammed Ali. He often continued his verbal abuse throughout the fight and the referees tolerated it. The football manager José Mourinho, formerly head coach of Chelsea and since returned is adept at this, which is a great shame as he is an excellent manager and these antics detract from the ethic of sport. However, since his return to Chelsea he seems to be rather more subdued. Athletes congregate in the holding room before being taken out to the event and someone might say something that sounds friendly, such as noting that an opponent needs to pay attention to an aspect of his style. This may make the person self-conscious and he will concentrate on what was said rather than running the race exactly as he had planned. Carl Lewis was not above the use of "mind games". He always came over at press conferences as most affable but those who competed against him found him rather less amiable. Before the runners were called to their blocks he would go down the line shaking hands with each in turn. To the casual observer this may seem very sporting but that is an illusion. In reality he was trying to intimidate them as if to say, "I'm the man. This is my race." The way that Usain Bolt plays to the crowd may be seen in a similar way. It may look like acknowledging the crowd who are basically the people who pay his fee but it also aims for psychological dominance over his opponents.

Carl Lewis was also on the receiving end of underhand tactics with innuendo about his sexuality. He never had a steady girlfriend, or boyfriend for that matter, but he said that was because he was so focussed on his career. He also did himself no favours with his choice of clothes that were often a trifle "Liberace". The American press were often hostile to him and called him "the flying faggot". This was not racism from a predominantly white press as other black athletes did not have the same trouble. He seemed arrogant and too focussed on money. He did not stay in the athletes' village and he was very reluctant to train with the relay team. In the 1988 Olympics, despite being the fastest American over 100 metres he was omitted from the relay team.

The legendary decathlon champion Daley Thompson liked his T-shirts. At a press conference after winning his gold medal in Los Angeles he wore a T-shirt with the caption "Is the world's second greatest athlete gay?" When questioned about it he told reporters that in England gay means happy. On the podium he wore a T-shirt that said, "Thanks America for a good Games and a great time" but on the back it said, "But what about the TV coverage?" The host country is responsible for the television coverage that is then released to all the competing nations. The coverage was so biased towards American competition that it was almost as if the rest of the world was just there to glorify them. The games were unusual in making a profit. The profit of $223 million was possible because of the $225 million paid by ABC for broadcasting rights and $4 million paid by each of 30 sponsors. They got what they paid for. The whole atmosphere was very chauvinistic and ultra-nationalistic. Many British people find the American way strange and uncomfortable. School children start the day by swearing allegiance to the flag and there is the hand on the heart during the national anthem. Most of us are happy just to stand. The little badge of the stars and stripes on the lapel of the American presidents' suits is curious. Is that in case no one knows who he is or where to send him if he gets lost? We showed national pride in 2012 with the Queen's diamond jubilee and a very successful Olympics, but the Americans seem more like a banana republic trying to find itself than a great nation that is confident and at ease.

In the sprint races everyone is on edge to get a good start that is so important over a short distance. A false start was sometimes used to upset the competition but since 2010 a single false start will result in disqualification. This seems rather harsh. On "get set" it is still possible to give a little twitch of the shoulder to give the impression of leaving the blocks and possibly getting an opponent to do a false start.

For decades there has been electronic timing rather than waiting for a human to press the button when he sees the starting gun fire. He had to press the button on seeing the smoke rather than hearing the bang as sound takes time to travel. The delayed human response was unreliable and made times seem faster than they really were. The first fully automatic timing when the starting gun starts the clock was as far back as the steeple chase in the 1928 Olympics. Such devices have been mandatory for world records to be accredited since 1977. Omega has been the official Olympic timer since 1932 and they have introduced electronic starting blocks. Omega's newest starting blocks measure the runner's reaction time by the pressure they exert against the foot pad rather than by movement. No one has a reaction time faster than one tenth of a second. The sensors in a starting block detect that a runner has exerted force on the pressure pads. If anyone moves out of the blocks in less than 0.1 or 10th of a second after the gun has fired it will read as a false start. The blocks can time to 0.001 or 1,000th of a second. If a sprinter rocks on his blocks he may give a fictitious false start. Even if an official comes and has words with him he may be expecting that whilst it has unsettled his opponents.

In football, as teams line up together to go through the tunnel before a match something said to an opponent may be designed to upset him and cause loss of concentration or perhaps to make him angry and to entice him into a foul tackle that will get a yellow or even red card. In the gentleman's game of cricket the Australians are adept at comments designed to upset the batsman. This is called "sledging". In the game for hooligans but played by gentlemen the English rugby team have used underhand techniques against the French. Their full-back was a very reliable kicker so, from the start of the game, the English team would kick up and under balls to be taken by the French full-back whilst the English pack would pile in on him. Before long he retaliated and was sent off.

If you are going to use underhand tactics to get a player sent off, at least be surreptitious about it. A classic example was the football game of England versus Portugal in the World Cup quarter final in 2006 when Wayne Rooney's short temper was exploited to get him sent off, aided and abetted by the Portugal players crowding around the referee insisting on dismissal. His Manchester United team mate Cristiano Ronaldo should at least have been discreet enough not to wink at his Portuguese team mates on the bench as if to say "Job done".

The term "Sledging" originates from a cricket match in Australia back in the 1960s. One of the teams learned that a member of the opposing team was having an affair with the wife of another member of his team. When the husband came out to bat the fielding team started to sing "When a man loves a woman" that was a great hit for Percy Sledge. That is the origin of the term "sledging".

In longer running races and in cycling there is organised boxing in of strong opponents but it is difficult for the authorities to have the evidence to take action. Often it seems to be viewed as just something that national and other teams do.

There was more than just bad sportsmanship in the Taekwondo in the 2008 Olympics in Beijing. When the Cuban Angel Matos received an injury and took more than the allowed minute for injuries he was disqualified in his bronze medal match against Kazakhstan. He pushed a judge and kicked the referee in the face, and then spat on the floor before being escorted out. His coach Leudis Gonzalez offered no apology, but accused the referee of being bribed by Kazakhstan. Both the competitor and his coach were given a lifetime ban from all world Taekwondo championships.

There is a new profession called sports psychologists. The successful sportsman has to have the right mental attitude to be able to compete at his best. He must believe in his ability to win. The person who goes out believing he will lose will certainly do so. In tennis it is essential to focus on the current point and to forget the silly mistake that lost the last one. Sportsmen are very superstitious and develop rituals such as which shoe they put on first. Anything that upsets their ritual can upset them and they must be able to cope. The sports psychologist will be able to develop a coping strategy with "mind games" but may also be well placed to plan them.

We have seen gross cheating from athletes and even from national bodies. We have seen bad sportsmanship and pushing the boundaries well beyond the altruistic nature of sport. We have even seen criminal activity and assault. It may be tempting to believe that it is the enormous financial rewards than players can earn that is behind such things, but cheating was rampant even in the days of the strict amateur. The urge to win is strong. We should remember Andy Warhol's observation about "famous for 15 minutes". However, the money is considerable and it depends on continued success. Dwayne Chambers, who will be mentioned later, is reputed to have received a salary of £200,000 a year but it would fall by 50% if he fell out of the top three in the world rankings. There is also the widely held belief that success at sport reflects well on the political system of the country of origin and shows that the country has a superior system to those who are less successful. We see this with China, the USA, the old Soviet Union and eastern bloc. North Korea can produce gold medallists at an Olympic Games as well as having a vast army and probably nuclear weapons, but it lacks the ability to feed its people.

Many people will go to great lengths to win at any cost. Sport is important. Sport is valuable. It gives health both mental and physical. It is war without the bloodshed. It is entertaining. Still it is only a game.

5. Performance Enhancing Substances

The story of performance enhancing substances in sport is long and interesting. In recent years there has been a constant battle between the agencies that try to detect doping and the people who aim to avoid exposure. The battle is prolonged and arduous and far from won. Discussion about drugs in sport can be very technical and difficult but descriptions here will be kept simple with explanation of any medical terms. Do not struggle with trying to pronounce the names of drugs and hormones as you read them. They are given for the sake of accuracy but most readers will never have heard of them and will find them very difficult to pronounce. Doctors love to rattle them off like a foreign language.

In the first part of the 20th century it was not unusual to find that perhaps two dozen runners started a marathon race, rather fewer than half finished and half of them required medical attention. Times have changed. The London Marathon is just one of many in the world today. The first London Marathon was held in 1981. There were more than 20,000 applications to run but only 6,747 were accepted and 6,255 crossed the finish line which is more than 92%. More recently there have been around 30,000 runners including elite athletes, club runners and many charity runners. Around 80% of all runners raise money for charities, some wearing silly costumes. Most finish. Fortunately few require medical attention for any serious matter.

In the 1904 Olympic marathon in St Louis, only 14 of the 27 starters finished and, as we have seen, Fred Lorz was disqualified for traveling part of the course in his trainer's car. The ultimate winner was Thomas Hicks who sustained himself with five raw eggs and brandy and he was periodically given injections of strychnine. Imagine a modern athlete receiving injections during the course of a race. He was helped across the finishing line and had the attention of four doctors.

Strychnine is a poison that is used to kill rodents but it was previously used as a "nerve tonic" as it stimulates the central nervous system. It causes apprehension and nervousness, and it can lead to convulsions and death. The doses used are unpleasant but not usually lethal. It is not to be recommended for a marathon or at any other time.

Having some sustenance on the way may seem like a good idea but if it is required, five eggs are not ideal. He probably thought that their high protein content would help his muscles but he would have done better to have loaded with carbohydrate the previous night to feed the muscles with glycogen to burn as glucose. Most marathon runners have pizza or pasta the night before a race. Eggs contain a significant amount of fat and protein which would have delayed stomach emptying considerably, as does exercise and he probably finished the race with most of the five eggs still undigested in his stomach.

Modern athletes like to drink in long distance races but not brandy. As exercise starts the muscles create heat that is dissipated by sweating and the body loses water. This will eventually lead to dehydration if not corrected. Blood flow to the kidneys is reduced as more goes to the muscles but the posterior pituitary gland in the brain also releases a substance called antidiuretic hormone (ADH) to make the kidneys produce more concentrated urine. Alcohol suppresses the release of ADH and so he would have produced a larger volume of urine than normal and this would have aggravated dehydration. It is probably dehydration that is a major cause of headache after a heavy night of alcohol consumption. There were water stations on the early marathon courses but they were few and far between. This was intentional to make the race more arduous.

Sam Mussabini, who was coach to Harold Abrahams among others, recommended strychnine to ward off tiredness. He also advocated cocaine lozenges. The Dangerous Drugs Act was yet to come. In 1903 Coca-Cola removed the cocaine from its drinks. Coke really did contain "coke". Another recommendation to astound the modern observer is that smoking was encouraged as it was thought to increase lung capacity. Obviously no one had tested the theory.

It is unsurprising that so few athletes completed the marathon and that many of those who did were in such a state. Knowledge of drugs and physiology had a long way to go.

STIMULANTS

Stimulants were banned by the International Association of Athletics Federations (IAAF) in 1928, but this was meaningless in the absence of testing. The governing bodies of cycling and football were the first to introduce drug testing in 1966. Testing in the Olympics started in 1968 in Mexico City.

The adverse effect of drugs in sport first reached public attention at the Rome Olympics in 1960. The Danish cyclist Knud Jensen died when he collapsed in the race and fractured his skull. They wore caps rather than cycle helmets then, so his head had no protection. He was pronounced dead at a nearby hospital. Cause of death was given as heat stroke but he was said to have taken eight pills of phenylisopropylamine and fifteen pills of amphetamine as well as coffee. All, including the caffeine in coffee, are stimulants. He had taken 25 pills in all. There was also Roniacol, a brand of nicotinyl alcohol which dilates blood vessels. The aim would have been to increase blood flow to muscles but, along with much else of the cocktail, it would have dilated many more blood vessels and dropped his blood pressure making him likely to faint. By far the best approach is to let the body's normal response to exercise increase the blood flow to muscles. As heat needs to be lost the blood flow to the skin will increase as will sweating. The body does the job very well without any drugs. The stimulants may even have induced him to press on in the heat of a summer in Rome when he would normally have slowed or stopped and so caused the heat stroke. The public was shocked by the death and there was a call to do something about drugs in sport. In 1967 there was an outcry again when the British cyclist Tom Simpson died in the Tour de France after taking amphetamines and alcohol. Alcohol also dilates blood vessels. It was a very hot day and the drugs may have contributed to his determination to continue when he should have stopped. He needed water and common sense, not stimulants.

Amphetamines and other stimulants are easy to detect as they have to be in the body at the time of competition to be of any value. Drugs that can be used to build muscles before a competition but then stopped whilst their benefit continues are much more difficult to control.

STEROIDS

The next group of drugs to reach public attention was the steroids. Steroids are a group of compounds that share a common basic chemical structure, but a slight change can make a great deal of difference in terms of their effect. They may be divided into the corticosteroids and the sex hormones. When patients are said to be on steroids this usually means corticosteroids that reduce inflammation. Cortisone is not often used today but similar, more potent compounds such as prednisolone or dexamethasone. There are also steroid creams for dermatitis. The corticosteroids can be used to reduce inflammation, to assist in recovery and to provide a burst of energy and create a temporary feeling of increased energy and well being. They are not used much in most sport but they are part of the enormous armoury of illegal drugs used in long distance road race cycling.

In sport or body building the word steroids usually means the anabolic steroids. These are steroids that build up muscle mass whilst the cortisone group or corticosteroids may be seen as catabolic steroids that break it down.

Male sex hormones are called androgens and female sex hormones are called oestrogens. Both sexes have both groups of hormones, but androgens predominate in men and oestrogens in women. Both groups of sex hormones are anabolic steroids as they help to build muscle but androgens are far more potent than oestrogens. This is why men are more muscular than women. Many people are amazed at how rapidly athletes can return to top class competition after pregnancy but they have had nine months of high female hormone levels. Jessica Ennis-Hill announced her withdrawal from the Commonwealth Games in 2014 because of pregnancy but her intention to defend her Olympic title in Rio in 2016. Physically there is no reason why she should not do so. In reality she may find the constraints of a family rather limiting. Many horrific stories of abuse of athletes have emerged from the old Soviet Bloc including stories of women being forced to get pregnant and then have an abortion to get benefit from the hormones. However, such stories have never been authenticated and they are unlikely to be true. The truth is probably that they became pregnant as a result of sexual abuse by their coaches.

Female athletes are allowed to take supplementary female hormones and many do. We call it "the pill". Oral contraceptives give a number of advantages. They are an extremely effective form of contraception, which is very important for fit young women. After being accepted for the London Marathon the commonest reason for not starting is pregnancy. Oral contraceptives tend to reduce premenstrual symptoms which may have an adverse effect on performance and they tend to reduce the blood loss of menstruation. They can also be used to change the date of menstruation so that it does not coincide with an important event. This is not cheating. This is common sense.

THE EARLY DAYS

The first people to try anabolic steroids in sport were probably the Ancient Greeks who ate the testicles of sheep. How effective they were is uncertain as the hormones would have been absorbed by the gut, transported to the liver and most would be inactivated by the liver. Natural sex hormones have to be given by injection.

Anabolic steroids were widely used after the Second World War to treat servicemen who had been in Japanese prisoner of war camps where they were treated abominably and the diet was grossly deficient in both calories and vitamins. The steroids helped them to build up their muscle mass again. Synthetic anabolic hormones were available in the 1920s and 1930s and they can be taken by mouth, but the systematic use in sport was not really until the 1960s.

The Soviet weightlifters used testosterone in the 1950s. It was noticeable how much more bulky they were than other competitors but also how much more hairy. When the Americans discovered this they felt that a synthetic hormone with more of the desired effects and fewer of the unwanted effects was required. The drug firm Ciba came up with methandrostenolone, better known by the trade name Dianabol. Initially it was regarded as safe and it had not yet been made illegal. However, athletes did not comply with the recommended dose but often took far more and it quickly gained disrepute.

Anabolic steroids are said to help to build strength and to delay fatigue. They are also said to reduce the recovery time from exhaustion. They allow training to be more intense. It is not only in events where strong muscles are required that they are used. A significant number of 800 metres runners have been banned for using anabolic steroids over the years. Anabolic steroids can cause liver disease including liver cancer and they may have an adverse effect on blood pressure and blood cholesterol raising the long term risk of heart attack or stroke. They lead to a reduction in the size and function of the testes. In women they cause masculine features to appear such as facial hair, male pubic hair distribution and a deeper voice. They can also affect the genitalia with enlargement of the clitoris. This and the deeper voice do not disappear on stopping the hormones. In both sexes they may build the strength of muscles but not tendons so that injuries increase. Other side effects of anabolic steroids include aggression, acne and hairiness. Some body builders take them not for competition but for vanity, to build muscle so that they are admired by others. In the 1970s I heard of a top judo player who took such drugs and then went home, smashed up the house and beat up his wife and children. No one admires a man who behaves like that.

Before the imposition of statutory controls of people in security jobs there were great problems with "bouncers" at night clubs. They would take steroids and work out in the gym by day and by night they would be on the doors of pubs until after 11pm and then clubs until 3am. They would take amphetamines to keep them awake and alert. With the aggression associated with steroids and the paranoia often caused by amphetamines it is unsurprising that these bouncers probably caused more trouble than they prevented.

By the 1970s anabolic steroids were so commonly used that many more were tempted to follow. The wisdom was that if you did not use them you could never win ahead of those who did. Be a user or a loser. However, it was 1974 by the time that reliable tests for anabolic steroids were available. The sports bodies introduced mandatory testing and failure to produce a sample on request was seen as a tacit admission of guilt. The trouble is that steroids can be stopped before the event but the muscle remains. Those who had access to sophisticated doping and testing expertise were told when to stop taking before an event. As already mentioned, the Soviet Bloc made cheating an art form and they excelled. Many others turned to the drugs without the back up. I was sad rather than angry in 1988 when Kerrith Brown of the British judo team at the Seoul Olympics was initially found to have a diuretic in his urine. A diuretic is a drug that makes the kidneys produce more urine. I assumed at first that he had failed to make the weight category and had used it to lose weight by losing water. Jockeys often do this. However, he had used it to dilute his urine to reduce the chance of an anabolic steroid being detected. Nandrolone, a synthetic steroid was later found. He obviously felt under great pressure. This was a very crude and unsophisticated attempt induced by the belief that it was the only way to succeed when so many others were using them too.

EAST AND WEST

Since the end of the cold war many stories have come out of the old Soviet Bloc about the systematic used of drugs in training camps. The athletes were told that they were vitamins or supplements but they knew otherwise from the effect they had. Discipline was strict and they could not refuse. The coaches had full state sponsored scientific backup to tell them when to give the drugs and when to stop them before competition. This was cheating on a grand state-endorsed and state-sponsored level. Although this was common in all the Eastern European countries and apparently in China today, the most systematic use of steroids and other such drugs came from East Germany. Despite a fairly small population, they suddenly became dominant in the 1970 and 1980s, especially in the power events.

However, it would be wrong to believe that the west was clean when it came to drugs and sport. In 1982 just before the Pan-American Games it was rumoured that new and better ways for testing for drugs had been introduced including the ability to detect steroid use up to a year before the test. This was untrue but 12 American athletes, mainly from the field events, returned home before the start of the games and many others sustained sudden and unexpected injuries which prevented them from competing. The Americans introduced drug testing before the 1984 Olympic Games in Los Angeles but many of the coaches and trainers used this not to weed out the athletes who took drugs, but to test the system to see how good it was, so as to be able to beat it. After the games the US Olympic Committee's chairman admitted that before the games 84 American athletes had tested positive, 10 of them at the Olympic trials but none was punished. There were also allegations that at the games paperwork was lost so that positive tests could not be traced back to the athletes.

There were stories of various tricks to bypass the system including surreptitiously giving some else's urine in the bottle. There are stories of East European women having a vaginal bag that they could squeeze to produce a specimen of urine that was not their own. Some women have told me that this is impossible, but perhaps East European power event women have muscles in places that other women do not. Another story was of a weightlifter who had a catheter passed into his bladder and his trainer's urine instilled so that he could produce a specimen of his trainer's urine instead of his own. He still tested positive. Nowadays the various conjuring tricks would be much more difficult to perform. Usually the first four athletes in an event are taken to the testing room to produce a sample but others can be chosen at random. They have to go there directly and are supervised on the way. They have a couple of hours in which to produce as they probably emptied their bladders before the event and they may be dehydrated after it. They may drink freely but they are not allowed out until they have produced a specimen and access of others to the room is strictly limited. The passing of the urine is directly witnessed by a same-sex official. They must be naked from the knees to the nipples. This alone is far more effective than the old "sex test" for rooting out any man who may wish to compete as a woman. With the athlete as a witness the urine specimen is split into two halves. The A specimen is sent to the laboratory for analysis and the B specimen is sealed and frozen in case findings in the A specimen need to be confirmed. They are labelled with a code and not with names or events. A senior official has access to the codes and if a result is positive the code is sent to the official to identify the person. The athlete may then ask for the B sample to be analysed in case there has been a technical error.

In his autobiography Mike Tyson claims to have used a false penis to outwit the authorities in Scotland to give a false, clean urine specimen. This was when he fought against Lou Savarese in 2000. He was not taking drugs to enhance performance but his chaotic lifestyle was one of recreational drug abuse. If this story is true it suggests that the "nipples to knees" rule was not applied. The book is called "*Undisputed Truth*" and is said to be his autobiography, but it would be surprising if someone with his limited literacy could write a book without considerable help or ghost authorship.

The mantra in the west was that drug abuse was limited to the eastern bloc but this was dealt another serious blow in 1988. The former British 400 metres athlete, David Jenkins, was sentenced to seven years in prison for conspiring to produce, smuggle and supply steroids. He was a well-educated man from Edinburgh who had gone to live in

California after marrying an American woman. He had used steroids himself and he was involved in an enormous project to supply illegal drugs. The prosecution said that his organisation was responsible for supplying 70% of the illegal steroids used in the USA. David Jenkins argues that this is a gross overestimate as if he was really supplying 70% of the market he would have dropped the price and taken 100% of the market.

Marita Koch was a very successful East German 400 metres runner who won the European Championships in 1978, 1982 and 1986 and the Moscow Olympics in 1980 before retiring in 1987. She was not in the 1984 Olympics because of the East European boycott. During her career she broke world records in 16 outdoor events and 14 indoor events. She never failed a drug test. After the Berlin Wall fell many East German athletes came under scrutiny. In 1991 several doctoral theses emerged along with other documents written by scientists working for the East German drug research programme. It was known as State Plan 14.25. The documents included lists of doses and timetables for the administration of anabolic steroids to many athletes of the former German Democratic Republic. This list included Marita Koch. It documented her use of the anabolic steroid Oral-Turinabol from 1981 to 1984. She always denied taking drugs, but a letter that she wrote to the head of the state-owned pharmaceutical company was discovered. Marita Koch complained that her teammate Bärbel Wöckel received larger doses of steroids than her because she had a relative who worked in the company. She was condemned by her own hand.

MASKING AGENTS

Allegations of the use of anabolic steroids are often based on an excessive improvement in performance. Teenagers may improve more rapidly than older athletes, just as a matter of maturation and this should be remembered when interpreting results. Michelle Smith was an Irish swimmer who improved considerably when she moved from Ireland to Holland to train. Not only did she have a new trainer but she could train in a 50 metres pool. At the time there was not a single 50 metres pool in all of Ireland. In Atlanta in 1996 she won three gold medals and a bronze in swimming events and all her tests were clear. However, she was in trouble in 1998 when she was accused of tampering with a urine sample when alcohol was found in it. This can be used as a masking agent to prevent illegal drugs from being detected. Further tests found androstenedione, a natural androgen like testosterone, in her urine and she was banned, but her disqualification was not retrospective to Atlanta. Hence her medals stood. Her husband and coach was Erik de Bruin who was a former Dutch discus thrower and shot putter who had been suspended after a failed drug test in 1993.

Athletes have found a number of ways to prevent detection of banned products and there are many websites that appear to offer authoritative advice to those who wish to cheat. Diuretics to make the kidneys produce more but dilute urine have been mentioned. The diuretics are also banned substances. Alcohol is a masking agent to prevent chemical detection and even green tea is recommended by some websites. Ben Johnson was alleged to have been treated for gonorrhea as he had probenecid in his urine. It was not yet banned for athletes but it was a valid part of some medical treatments. It increases the excretion of uric acid by the kidneys, reducing blood levels of uric acid and the risk of attacks of acute gout. It also decreases the excretion of penicillin. At the time the standard treatment for gonorrhea was a high dose of penicillin along with probenecid to make the penicillin last longer. Probenecid can also be used to block the excretion of steroids by the kidneys so that they do not appear in the urine. This was the implication of the finding.

There is a constant battle between the regulatory authorities with the testing agencies and the athletes with their coaches. Sir Arthur Gold was a former British shot put champion as well as holding many senior posts in athletics including chairman of the Commonwealth Games Council and chairman of the British Olympic Association. He was an ardent campaigner for more stringent drugs testing but even he admitted that it is only the careless and the ill-advised who will be caught.

CHINESE WHISPERS

In the 1990s the Chinese teams had a very bad time of getting caught at international events despite having no positive tests on home soil. In swimming their mighty and powerful women were shocking the world whilst their men were not doing so spectacularly well. Women would benefit more from anabolic steroids than men as they produce less natural anabolic steroids. In the 1994 Asian Games, China won twenty-three gold medals but had to return nine of them after positive tests. This included both men and women.

Pictures of the Chinese women's swimming medley team from the 1990s are quite fascinating. Not only were they all extremely heavily built but all four had gross acne. Acne is a side effect of anabolic steroids. If only one had such acne we may say that the poor girl had an unfortunate complexion, but for all four to have it so badly shouts, "Anabolic steroids!" They also had swimsuits that were brief at the groin, as was the current style, and all had needed to shave a male distribution of pubic hair. The breast stroke swimmer and world champion who powered her way through the water was nicknamed "the dump truck". Her style was so bad that my daughters observed that if anyone was to swim breast stroke like that at a Yorkshire junior meet she would be disqualified for having such a bad style. To be the best in the world requires many attributes and this normally includes an excellent style.

The Chinese swimmer Ye Shewen was just 16 years old at the 2012 London Olympics. This teenage sensation does not look as grossly "pumped up" as her predecessors but she does not look like a normal 16 years old girl. She was also associated with allegations of steroid use although none was proved. Her performance in the 400 metres individual medley was so outstanding that it raised questions. She knocked a full second off the world record and five seconds off her personal best. She swam the final 50 metres faster than the American gold medal winner Ryan Lochte in the men's medley finals. He was 27-years-old, male, 15 centimetres (6 inches) taller and about 20 kg (3st 2lbs) heavier.

She did not fail any drugs test but neither did Marita Koch. China may simply be playing smarter rather than cleaner.

Shortly before the 2012 London Olympics Dr Xue Yinxian, retired chief medical supervisor for the Chinese gymnastics team in the 1980s, is reported to have said that in the 1980s and 1990s drug use in Chinese sport was rampant. Its top sports official told a meeting in October 1978 that performance-enhancing drugs were simply new things that should be utilised, provided they were properly understood. They were regarded as simply scientific training. The situation was so bad that before the 2000 Olympics, Chinese athletes had to submit to blood as well as urine tests. Chinese swimming went into decline but has since resurged although the allegations of doping remain. They may just be more cunning and devious in how they do it. After the fall of the Berlin Wall in 1989 it was rumoured that some East German doctors were seen in China. This coincided with their rise to power as a sporting nation. China was supposed to have promised to clean up its act as a condition of hosting the 2008 Olympics but that might mean just not getting caught.

THE BEN JOHNSON SAGA

The Canadian sprinter Ben Johnson is probably the best known and most reviled of athletes who have tested positive for anabolic steroids. In Seoul in 1988 he won the gold medal in the 100 metres, beating Carl Lewis and Linford Christie and setting a new world record. However, he tested positive for stanazolol and was disqualified from both the medal and the world record.

The story surrounding this race and its aftermath is fascinating. After the race Ben Johnson went to the testing room as required but he took some time to produce his specimen as he had passed urine before the race and he was dehydrated. He sat in the room drinking cans of beer that were given to him by a man who should not have been there. He was later identified as André Jackson, a man who was close to the Carl Lewis camp. It was said that Carl Lewis knew nothing about this but his trainer, Joe Douglas had obtained a pass to get him in. The rationale was to watch Ben Johnson to make sure that he did not take any masking agents. Ben Johnson drank about six cans of beer before he could produce his specimen and he was really quite inebriated by the time he gave his press conference afterwards. A number of journalists have spoken to André Jackson in the years since he was identified as the mystery man and they have asked him if he tampered with Ben Johnson's drink to produce the positive result. He seems never to have confirmed or to have denied it. A pertinent question to ask both Ben Johnson and André Jackson is if the cans of beer were handed over intact or if the seal was broken. If the widget was intact it would have been virtually impossible to have contaminated it. If the widget had been opened this would give ample opportunity.

The story around the 100 metres final in the Seoul Olympics is so broad and intriguing that the sports writer Richard Moore has written a whole book about it, which he has called "*The dirtiest race in history*". Six of the eight finalists, including Carl Lewis have tested positive for drugs at some time. However, it was not just the drug use that made it dirty.

According to Richard Moore, the response of Charlie Francis, Ben Johnson's coach, when he found that he had tested positive for stanazolol was that he did not want his athletes on stanazolol on race day as it tightens them up. As far as he was concerned Ben Johnson had taken steroids but he had stopped them long enough before the race for them not to be detected. He also said that his athletes were on estragol, not stanazolol. Jamie Astaphan, the doctor with the Johnson camp denied to Charlie Francis that Ben Johnson could have taken stanazolol. An Internet search for estragol finds that it is a natural organic compound that is extracted from basil and it is used in perfumes and as a food additive for flavour. Estragon is also another name for the herb tarragon. However, a bottle of the substance called estragol from Ben Johnson's doctor, Jamie Astaphan, was analyzed a few years later and found to be Winstrol V. This is a preparation of stanazolol used in veterinary practice to increase the meat on animals before slaughter. An Internet search for Winstrol

V shows that it is readily available online and it is often abused by body builders. It should be available solely by prescription of a vet. There is no suggestion online of the use of estragol as an anabolic steroid and its chemical structure is not that of a steroid. Did the doctor really not know what he was giving?

If a synthetic steroid such as nandrolone or stanazolol is found there is no question that the individual has taken an illegal substance. However, it was not until after the 1984 games that it was possible to test for stanazolol. Athletes turned to testosterone, which is a natural substance found normally in the human body, with higher levels in men than women. The problem for the testing agencies is to decide what a normal level is and what constitutes evidence of doping. Normal blood levels vary considerably between individuals. The solution is to look at another hormone that is also normal in the body and to compare the ratio of the two. Usually the hormone epitestosterone is used as the reference although sometimes androstenolone which is also known as dehydroepiandrosterone (DHEA) or prasterone is used. Under normal circumstances, the ratio of testosterone to DHEA should be no more than 4:1. The ratio of testosterone to epitestosterone or T:E ratio is normally 1:1 or 2:1 but should be no more than 6:1. If it is between 6:1 and 10:1 further consideration will be given. After the 1988 Olympics Ben Johnson was banned for two years, but after his return in 1993 he had an unacceptable T:E ratio and was banned for life. He was said to have used many other synthetic anabolic steroids including furazabol, which had previously been undetectable.

Another athlete who fell foul of the T:E ratio was Mary Decker who was an 800 metres runner. In 1996 she had a test with a ratio of greater than six but she denied taking drugs and said that perhaps her oral contraceptives had caused the problem. She took the case to arbitration but the panel, no doubt receiving expert advice, rejected her appeal.

In 2007 Floyd Landis was stripped of his title as winner of the Tour de France and given a two year ban from professional racing after a T:E ratio of 11. Another test that is sometimes used in deciding if borderline cases represent natural or pharmacological testosterone involves look-ing at the ratio of two isotopes of carbon. A technically sophisticated test called gas chromatography is used to determine to ratio of ^{13}C and ^{12}C. Both are carbon atoms but the former has one neutron more and hence an atomic weight of 13 instead of 12. A low ratio of ^{13}C to ^{12}C is said to imply that the testosterone came from outside the body and therefore was taken illegally. This is a very sophisticated and very expensive test.

SUPPLEMENTS

In the 1990s and early 2000s the testing agencies found many positive results for the steroid nandrolone. Often the athletes denied having taken it but the source was tracked down to nutritional supplements that contained it. This is not a natural substance but a synthetic steroid. Professor Wilhelm Schaencer of the IOC laboratory in Cologne performed a two year study of nutritional supplements and found that many contained this illegal substance although it was not included in the list of ingredients. Of the first 100 batches that he tested 16 proved positive for nandrolone.

The Bay Area Laboratory Cooperative was based in San Francisco and was supposed to be a company that sold supplements to athletes. In 2002 a federal investigation of BALCO and its owner, Victor Conte, began. They were accused of supplying performance enhancing drugs to Major-league Baseball players and other athletes from 1988. Their speciality was a steroid called Tetrahydrogestrinone (THG) that was undetectable at the time. Hence it was known as "the clear". The business had started in 1984 to sell nutritional supplements and vitamins. Its owner had no qualifications in nutrition. This is not exceptional for people who call themselves "nutritionists". A chemist from Illinois called Patrick Arnold produced the drugs and Victor Conte developed a cycle of drug taking that included erythropoietin, human growth hormone, modafinil, testosterone cream, and tetrahydrogestrinone (THG). Erythropoetin and growth hormone will be discussed later. Modanafil is described as a "wakefulness inducing drug". The American

Food and Drug Agency have licensed it for the treatment of narcolepsy and excessive daytime drowsiness. A syringe containing THG was sent anonymously to the director of the Los Angeles Olympic Analytical Laboratory and he developed a test for the substance. He tested 550 existing samples from athletes, of which 20 proved to be positive for THG. Of the British athletes involved the one with the most high profile was the sprinter Dwayne Chambers. The service offered included a personalised drug regime and testing to make sure that all was clear. This is said to have cost Dwayne Chambers $30,000 a year. There is obviously an air of scientific credibility surrounding this business but as it was run by a nutritionist with no qualifications in nutrition we may wonder how scientifically robust it really was.

The sport that suffered most from the BALCO revelations was baseball which was the only major sport at the time that did not have a steroids policy. It now has one but it is still criticised for being too lax.

The BALCO organisation was wound up and Victor Conte served four months in prison before pleading guilty. He is now a free man who runs a business called "Scientific Nutrition for Advanced Conditioning" (SNAC). Many believe that he has opened a similar organisation with a different name. The name may include the words "scientific nutrition" but he has still not obtained any recognised qualification in the science of nutrition.

OTHER HORMONES

Human Chorionic Gonadotrophin (HCG) is produced by the placenta in the first 16 weeks of pregnancy. It helps to maintain the pregnancy by inducing the ovary to produce the hormone progesterone. In males it stimulates the testes to produce more testosterone whilst keeping the T:E ratio normal. However, it is probably not very effective as follicle stimulating hormone (FSH) is responsible for maintaining the volume of the testes. In females it would have no benefit. In males it can lead to breast enlargement called gynaecomastia. In combination with anabolic steroids it can cause headaches, depression and general swelling from water retention called oedema. Taking anabolic steroids may cause atrophy of the testes, meaning that they shrink as the driving hormone from the pituitary gland (FSH) has been suppressed by the steroids. Hence HCG may be used to help the body restart its natural androgen production by getting the testes working again. Ben Johnson was also said to have tested positive for HCG in 1988.

Another hormone that is sometimes used is human growth hormone (HGH or hGH), also called somatotrophin. It is produced by the pituitary gland and is important for the normal growth of children. Athletes like it because it is said to increase muscle mass whilst also breaking down fat stores. Hence the person hopes to become more muscular with less body fat. It is also said to accelerate muscle recovery after training, allowing more intense training. Sometimes a tumour of the pituitary gland can lead to excessive production of growth hormone. If this happens before the growing ends of bones have fused at puberty it will cause gigantism. If it happens after puberty it causes a condition called acromegaly. There are large hands and feet, a broad nose and the chin extends rather like the old Mr Punch. Some athletes have been found to have widening jaws and loosening teeth as a result of self-induced acromegaly. This does not reverse on stopping the hormone.

HGH for treating children with growth hormone deficiency used to be obtained from the pituitary glands of dead bodies. Small amounts were obtained from each gland and the output was pooled. In the 1980s it was found that new variant Creutzfeldt–Jakob disease (nvCJD), the infection linked to BSE or "mad cow disease" was being transmitted by this route. The NHS stopped using this source and for a year no HGH treatment was given until HGH from recombinant DNA technology (genetic engineering) became available. There are a number of websites which claim that various foods or herbs can increase the natural production of HGH. However, I have been unable to find any scientific evidence that this has any significant effect. The marketing of such products along with promotion from "health" and "training" websites is never affected by lack of scientific data.

There is another hormone that may be similar to HGH in effect although its efficacy is disputed. It is Insulin-like Growth Factor (IGF-1) and is produced by the liver. It does not appear to be widely used.

A hormone that is well known but not widely recognised to be associated with abuse is insulin. It is the hormone that is injected by millions of diabetics every day. It aids the active transport of glucose from the blood into the muscles where it is laid down as glycogen. This also lowers blood glucose. This is well known, but what is less widely known is that insulin also helps to transport amino acids, the building blocks of protein, into the muscle cells. For athletes it serves two purposes. It can be used to prevent the breakdown of muscle after anabolic steroids have been stopped. It also pushes glucose into the muscle to be stored as glycogen which is muscle fuel for future use. Insulin has to be given by injection as it is a protein that would be digested if taken by mouth. If insulin is being given to someone who is not diabetic there should be intravenous glucose administration too and it should be monitored by a doctor. The cyclist Tyler Hamilton is someone who used insulin, but did not like it as it made him sweat profusely. If a diabetic has too much insulin and blood glucose is too low he will have sweating, palpitations and a feeling of anxiety. Glucose is actively transported into muscle by insulin but it has to diffuse into the brain and so if the blood level falls the brain will be starved of glucose. Muscles can burn glucose or fats but the brain can use only glucose. The person may become aggressive and uncoordinated with slurred speech. A more severe reduction in blood glucose called hypoglycaemia can result in convulsions and even death.

A SUPER WHEEEZE

The drug clenbuterol is supposed to be of value for asthma. It is similar to salbutamol which is the commonest drug in inhalers for asthma but it has never been licenced for use. However, it is also said to have anabolic and fat burning properties, rather like HGH and some weight-lifters have been found to have clenbuterol in their urine. Their excuse was that that they had felt tightness in the chest whilst training and so they had acquired it to treat self-diagnosed asthma. This begs the question, if you were a weightlifter in competitions, and you thought you had asthma, would you see your doctor or the team doctor or would you buy medication that is not licenced for asthma, but it is in "the steroid users' black book"? Doctors involved with sport are very aware of how careful they have to be with what they prescribe. Even doctors who are not keen on sport can look in the back of the British National Formulary and see a list of banned drugs. Clenbuterol is not licenced for use in humans but it can readily be bought over the Internet. It has also found favour with beef farmers in China and Mexico and hence small amounts of this drug may appear in meat from those countries. During the 2010 Tour de France, the winner Alberto Contador tested positive for a minute quantity of clenbuterol. He blamed it on having eaten a contaminated steak that originated from Spain. The amount of clenbuterol in his urine was so small it was unlikely to have affected his performance but after two years of hearings the Court of Arbitration in Sport banned him for two years, also stripping him of his titles for the Tour de France 2010, Giro d'Italia 2011 and several other races. Clenbuterol is said to increase aerobic capacity which means the amount of oxygen the body can use during physical exercise. It improves the body's ability to transport oxygen and to metabolise fat. Because of the last it has been hailed as a potential aid to weight loss aid and to increase lean muscle mass.

ERYTHROPOIETIN

Red blood cells contain haemoglobin, which carries oxygen around the body. Hence having more haemoglobin is an advantage, especially for endurance athletes. However, too many red blood cells will increase the viscosity of the blood so that it is thick, rather like cold engine oil. Until this state is reached, a higher level of haemoglobin is beneficial. High levels of red blood cells plus dehydration may make blood very thick so that it forms a sludge and it blocks arteries. It is thought that this may account for some sudden unexplained deaths in cyclists.

There are three ways that higher haemoglobin levels can be achieved. One is legal. Two are illegal.

The first way is called blood doping. It involves taking a unit of blood, which is about a pint or half a litre from the athlete about six weeks before the event. This is stored and over those six weeks the body makes up the lost blood. The day before the event the taken unit of blood is transfused back into the athlete to give him a higher level of haemoglobin. Sometimes the athlete receives a donor's blood rather than providing his own. Before anyone receives blood in hospital it is cross-matched which means that it is checked to make sure that there will not be a severe reaction if it is transfused. Failure to do so could have serious results. Simply transfusing from someone else in the entourage with the same blood group could cause such problems and, unlike the blood transfusion service, they may not check for diseases that could be spread by transfusion.

The legal way to raise haemoglobin values is to train at altitude. The lower pressure of oxygen in the air makes the kidneys produce a hormone called erythropoietin which increases red blood cell production. Training at altitude is expensive for those who have to train abroad and rapid ascent without acclimatisation can lead to mountain sickness that can be fatal. Kenyan athletes train at altitudes in their homeland. The athletes return to low level before the event but they still have a high level of haemoglobin and a high oxygen carrying capacity.

Erythropoietin (EPO) is produced by the kidneys. It stimulates the bone marrow to produce more red blood cells. It is now produced by genetic engineering, more correctly called recombinant DNA technology. It is very useful in patients with chronic kidney failure who are anaemic because of lack of erythropoietin. It avoids giving blood transfusions which contain white blood cells as well as red. They may sensitise the patients to tissue antigens and cause them to reject a transplanted kidney. It may also be useful for patients with cancer. EPO was first used by athletes in the 1980s but it was not until 2000 that it was possible to detect it. Testing was introduced for the Sydney Olympics and it involved both a blood and urine test. In 2003 a urine test alone was accepted. It is based on particles of the recombinant EPO being found in the urine. However, there have been suggestions that false positives may occur after very strenuous exercise. If in doubt, probably a blood test and a urine test would be required. This is a difficult test but EPO users can be caught and they have been caught.

There is a problem with long term use of erythropoietin in that the body may become dependent upon the injections. Hence a new drug has been developed called CERA which stands for Continuous Erythropoiesis Receptor Activator. It is called a third generation drug after EPO and the second generation erythropoiesis-stimulating agents. Erythropoiesis means stimulation of red blood cell production. Used clinically it is given just once a month. It was first detected in riders in the Tour de France in 2008. It can be detected and this is yet another test to be added to the list of tests. It can be detected in blood and after exercise in urine.

It was sometime after the 2012 Olympics that the cycling world was rocked by the news that its great star Lance Armstrong had been a persistent user of performance enhancing drugs. He was a hero who at 25 was diagnosed with testicular cancer and was told that his chance of surviving was less than 40%. He had treatment, overcame his cancer and went on to become an extremely successful professional road racing cyclist who won the Tour de France a record seven consecutive times between 1999 and 2005. The sport has a bad reputation for doping and he constantly had to deny allegations despite never having had any positive test in the approximately 600 drug tests he has taken over his cycling career.

Road race cycling is a most arduous sport and competitors may burn as much as 9,000 calories a day during a race. This may be difficult to consume in a day of racing and there are stories of cyclists sleeping with a tube into their stomach to feed them whilst they sleep. This is not illegal. Lance Armstrong said that almost everyone was using erythropoietin to boost blood levels and lied about it in the late 1990s. In June 2012, the United States Anti-Doping Agency (USADA) accused Lance

Armstrong of both taking and trafficking of drugs. This was based on blood samples from 2009 and 2010, and supported by statements from witnesses including former teammates. He was also said to have put pressure on teammates to take unauthorized performance-enhancing drugs. He is alleged to have used EPO, testosterone, corticosteroids and various substances to mask positive test results. He was banned from participating in sports sanctioned by the World Anti-doping Agency (WADA). He publicly admitted to the allegations in an interview on television in January 2013. The next Tour de France in the summer of 2013 was won by British cyclist Chris Froome, the second ever British rider to win, the other being Bradley Wiggins the previous year. However, he was very frustrated at all the questions he had to face about doping rather than being hailed as a British triumph for the second consecutive year. It seems that all too often the hacks prefer a hate story to good news.

Back in 2004 *The Sunday Times* printed an article alleging that Lance Armstrong used drugs. He sued them and was awarded £300,000 in damages. In 2013, after the truth came out, *The Sunday Times* returned to the High Court to seek the return of the £300,000 plus legal fees of more than £700,000, in total more than £1million. This shows again that regardless of the outcome of a case the winners are always the lawyers. An out-of-court settlement was reached, the details of which were confidential.

OTHER DRUGS

Beta blockers are basically an anti-adrenaline drug. They stop the heart from beating so fast and for athletes in performance events they would be totally counterproductive. However, they can also reduce any slight tremor or shake. Hence they are also on the list of banned substances as they would give an advantage in shooting events. They are also banned in snooker.

Athletes can be in trouble for taking "recreational" drugs such as cannabis. It is of no value to performance and it may be detected in the urine for a fortnight after use and longer in habitual users. The justification is that athletes are role models for young people. This also applies to footballers who have tested positive for cannabis or cocaine. However, if the tests were not done, no one would know that their heroes take recreational drugs and so they would not be a bad example. It is the testing that makes them a bad example. The American Judoka Nicholas Delpopolo was expelled from the London Olympics for a positive test for cannabis. He claimed to have inadvertently eaten some cake that contained it. One commentator noted that although the motto of the Olympic Games is "Faster, higher, stronger", it did not mean "high" in that sense.

Mike Tyson became the youngest heavyweight boxing world champion in 1986 at the age of 20. In his autobiography "*Undisputed Truth*" he says that the drug abuse continued after that, even sometimes up to the time of a fight. It seems likely that the notorious fight against Evander Holyfield in 1997 was also a time of drug taking. This saw Tyson bite a piece out of Holyfield's ear. He used cocaine and cannabis and on one occasion tested positive for the latter and was fined $200,000. He also admits to being an alcoholic. He likens his drug use to that of generals, saying, "The history of war is the history of drugs. Every great general and warrior from the beginning of time was high." Generals have to make logical and sensible decisions. Any general who was intoxicated with drugs would not last long.

Generally speaking, the concern in sport is with performance enhancing drugs but these recreational drugs offer no benefit and can have an adverse effect on performance.

HOW BIG IS THE PROBLEM?

Obviously, it is impossible to know how many athletes do take drugs of various sorts. According to WADA between one and two percent of elite athletes give positive results but that is only those who are caught. Research from Germany found that 13% of recreational athletes admitting to taking performance enhancing substances such as steroids and growth hormone. In addition they asked about cognitive doping which means taking substances to improve mental function. The athletes would be hoping for faster responses or greater concentration. There were 15% who admitted to that. These substances include caffeine in high doses as well as amphetamines and drugs such as methylphenidate (trade name Ritalin) and modafinil. Methylphenidate is used to treat attention deficit hyperactivity disorder (ADHD) and modafinil is used to treat narcolepsy. Both are prescription only medicines. Their effectiveness and potential dangers in such cases are unknown. In baseball, up to eight percent of major league players have been diagnosed with ADHD which probably represents an enormous amount of fraudulent diagnosis to justify illicit drugs. Amphetamines, methylphenidate, modafinil and even caffeine in excess are banned substances.

There are a lot of people taking a lot of stuff. Often they are taking multiple drugs without supervision or with unskilled supervision and the effects may be lethal. Not all these people are professional sportsmen. We need to protect athletes from themselves.

WHERE NEXT?

We may ask what will be the next step in performance enhancement after the various hormones. The answer is probably a technique called gene doping. Genetic modification is well established. This is how the bacterium E coli can be used to synthesis human insulin, EPO, human growth hormone and many other substances too. It may be possible to insert genes into human beings and this has vast potential for treating serious diseases such muscular dystrophy, haemophilia, cystic fibrosis and some genetic causes of blindness. The opportunities for curing some diseases are very exciting but this is for the future. However, it is feared that gene doping may be tried to improve athletic performance and it may be difficult to detect. One possible use is to introduce genes which produce higher levels of IGF-1 which is important in the growth and development of musculoskeletal structures. Insulin-like Growth Factor (IGF-1) has been briefly mentioned already. This would help injured athletes to repair damaged tissues such as muscles, tendons or ligaments more rapidly.

WADA believes that detection will be difficult but possible. The technique is likely to look for the consequences of gene doping in blood samples rather than the transfer of genes. Certain enzymes and proteins may be present in increased amounts. Another possibility is the use of MRI scans to detect areas of unusual gene expression.

Effects on performance would be varied but could be substantial. There are many types of gene that could be transferred, depending upon what attributes were desired. Improved endurance, muscle strength and size, and faster recovery from injury and fatigue are all possibilities. At present side effects of gene transfer are unclear but it would be most unwise to assume that they would not exist.

6. Getting Caught

When a positive test occurs there are occasions when the athlete will immediately admit it but these tend to be a minority. Generally speaking, the mantra is to deny and deny until it becomes simply impossible.

In 1988 Carl Lewis was caught on a positive drug test, not for steroids but for the stimulants ephedrine, pseudoephedrine and phenylpropanolamine. This could be the contents of a cough mixture. Carl Lewis claimed that he thought that he may have asthma and so he bought a Chinese herbal remedy called *ma huang* used to treat asthma, hay fever and the common cold. The US Olympic Committee accepted that he had taken it inadvertently and so let him off with a warning. This excuse seems as poor as that of the weight lifters who took clembuterol. Why did he not go to his personal doctor about his diagnosis of asthma? If it was real he could have prescribed an inhaler that is not a banned substance and, unlike herbal remedies, it has been scientifically tested to show that it works. If this was truly innocence it again highlights how many people think that herbal remedies will give them something safe and effective compared with scientific medicine. In fact many people may have found that it does work, but because of the pharmacological substances that were added rather than the herbs. Contamination of Chinese remedies and supplements by pharmaceutical products is a real and common problem. They are not licenced as medicines and so they do not have the same restrictions. Nevertheless, in the UK it is illegal to sell a supplement that is contaminated with a prescription only medicine. In this case they were not prescription only medicines and it was not in the UK.

Linford Christie also tested positive for pseudoephedrine after the 200 metres in the 1988 Olympics. He blamed ginseng tea that had been contaminated and he was lucky to escape a ban. The committee accepted his story of unintended use by a majority of just one. Once again we see the problem of pharmaceutical agents in Chinese herbal preparations and the assumption that these substances are innocuous but beneficial.

On other occasions the excuses that are given are quite imaginative but as more evidence emerges there is really little option but to confess and the explanations previously offered seem ever more disingenuous. We have seen several excuses already including:

- It must be anabolic steroids from the meat I ate.
- It must be my contraceptive pill.
- Someone must have given me some cake spiked with cannabis.
- I thought that I might have asthma so I bought a drug that is not licenced for asthma but it is in the *steroid users' black book*.
- Carl Lewis gave a similar excuse about asthma for taking a herbal preparation laced with stimulants.
- Linford Christie blamed a Chinese herbal teas for a banned stimulant.

We have also seen some great excuses from allegations unrelated to drugs:

- Going round the marathon course in a car was only a joke and not intended to defraud.
- I ran the first 35 kilometres of the marathon barefoot for health reasons and put on my trainers for just the last seven kilometres.

Occasionally the athlete will be nonchalant about the cheating, especially if he does not face disciplinary action. Perhaps the most obvious example was from the Football World Cup quarter-final, England versus Argentina in 1986. Diego Maradona used his hand to deflect the ball into the England net but the referee failed to see it and gave the winning goal. Video replay was quite clear and it can still be seen on YouTube today. Maradona was quite unabashed and seemed proud of his cunning, or as anyone with any decency would call it cheating. He called it "partly the hand of Maradona, partly the hand of God". When he had scored, or at least put the ball in the net, his team-mates were unenthusiastic as they had seen the foul even if the referee had not. He told them to crowd round and congratulate him before the referee realised that something was amiss. In 2013, still basking in his ignominy, he said that it was again the hand of God that had led to the election of an Argentinian pope. How the Pope felt about having his election compared to a notorious example of cheating is not recorded.

There are many ingenious excuses for why an athlete had a positive test. Sometimes the governing authorities seem to be incredibly gullible and eager to overturn a ban. Other times they just raise their eyebrows as if to say, "You're having a laugh." It is a matter of luck which group an individual meets and there is no uniformity of approach. The problem is that the officials of a national organisation are most reluctant to ban their own stars. This is unsurprising and it is a big problem. Here is a list of a number of athletes and the less plausible explanations that they gave:

- In 1998 the tennis player Petra Korda tested positive for nandrolone, an anabolic steroid, which he claimed must have been from veal that he ate. The Association of Tennis Professionals calculated that he would have had to eat 40 calves a day for 20 years to achieve the levels of drug found in his body. He was banned for just a year but never ceased to maintain his innocence. Perhaps his coach was giving it to him without his knowledge.

- The sprinter Justin Gatlin tested positive for steroids but claimed that his masseur must have sabotaged him by using a cream containing a steroid. There had been arguments about money.

- Dieter Baumann, a German 5.000 metres runner claimed that his toothpaste had been spiked with steroid.

- The cyclist Tyler Hamilton had a positive test for blood doping. It was not his own blood but that of a donor that had been transfused.

This required the connivance of a doctor. He admitted that on another occasion he had been infused with his own blood, but by another cyclist, not a doctor. He also used EPO and various other drugs. When he tested positive for the anabolic steroid DHEA he said that it was for depression. DHEA is not licenced for depression and no doctor would prescribe it for the condition, especially to an athlete. If he really did have depression he could have seen his doctor for something legal and effective. The DHEA was part of a "vitamin supplement" that he took for depression. Vitamins do not cure depression either.

- The French tennis player Richard Gasquet tested positive for cocaine. He appealed against suspension to the International Tennis Federation and explained that it was after a night out in Miami where he had kissed a girl who had been taking cocaine and that is how it was transferred. The tribunal accepted his plea saying, "This explanation is more likely than not to be the correct one."

- Javier Sotomayor, a Cuban high jumper tested positive for cocaine after winning a gold medal at the Pan-American Games in 1999. Fidel Castro went on television to defend him with a passionate speech accusing the CIA and the "well-known Cuban-American mafia" of conspiring against the athlete as part of their counter-revolution.

- In 1992 a Spanish runner called Daniel Plaza tested positive for the steroid nandrolone and he explained that he had recently performed an epic oral sex session with his pregnant wife. Pregnant women have high levels of certain sex steroids but nandrolone is a synthetic hormone that women do not produce in pregnancy or at any other time. However, further tests showed no signs of the hormone in his body although normally it would take much longer for it to disappear. In 2006, he won a court case that cleared his name of wrongdoing.

- Dennis Mitchell was a successful American sprinter but in 1992 he tested positive for testosterone. He attributed this to a marathon sex session the previous night as it was his wife's birthday and "The lady deserves a treat." USA Track and Field accepted his explanation, but the IAAF did not, so he was banned for two years.

When athletes who have tested positive protest their innocence it is very easy to be cynical about it, especially when so many start by protesting their innocence before eventually admitting to a lifestyle of systematic drug taking. However, some are so vehemently adamant about their innocence for so long that it is tempting to believe that if they were taking illegal substances it was without their connivance. Coaches may be surreptitiously administering substances in food or drink but not via injection. In July 2013 the sprinters Asafa Powell and Tyson Gay both tested positive for the stimulant oxilifrine and both blamed supplements given by members of their training team without their knowledge. Both may be right.

Top class athletes often take supplements of various types. In a business in which 0.1% of performance can make so much difference they need every advantage they can gain. Most of us do not need any food supplements if we eat a varied and healthy diet. Athletes have much greater physical needs during the day but that also means that they need to eat more to provide the calories and the evidence that supplements are needed is not compelling. However, getting athletes or their coaches to acknowledge that is not easy. Trainers, nutritionists and physiotherapists may have few or dubious qualifications. Just because of regime sounds very scientific does not mean that it is. Travis Tygart, the CEO of the US Anti-doping Agency says, "There are a lot of snake-oil salesmen who end up taking advantage of the athletes." Supplements are not always extra vitamins or minerals but may include various herbs and other concoctions. This can easily be the source of trouble. People are naïve enough to believe that herbs are legal, safe and effective but scientific testing for efficacy and safety has not been done.

An interesting vitamin that athletes often like is vitamin B12. It is required for making red blood cells and severe deficiency can also cause problems with nerves. There are some diseases that can cause vitamin B12 deficiency and these are by far the commonest causes but they are rare in top class athletes. The vitamin is very common in many foods and getting a dietary deficiency is extremely difficult although a strict vegan may just manage. Once any deficiency has been corrected a person with one of these diseases needs an injection of the vitamin just once every three months. Judging from various parametres of the blood, there is no apparent benefit from giving injections more often. However, patients do sometimes claim that they feel better after the injection and they want it every month or more often. Athletes also feel better after the injection. It seems likely that the little pink injection has a very potent placebo effect, as no one has been able to demonstrate anything more concrete about it. In other words, it is of psychological benefit which is all in the mind but the placebo effect can be very potent. There seems to something euphoric and almost addictive about vitamin B12 injections.

The use of steroids or antibiotics in meat production is a source for concern in the general population and debate is needed about the ratio of benefits to risks. However, it does not seem that they are truly a cause for innocent positive drug tests. It is quite possible that athletes could have received banned drugs inadvertently, especially if given by a member of the coaching team. Chinese herbal supplements are no more drug free than the Chinese sporting teams.

Where international athletes are concerned it is important that decisions to bar or to forgive are made by unprejudiced members of an international body. It is not fair to ask national officials to consider banning their own stars.

Whilst we may laugh at some of the excuses that are given, they suggest a culture of lie and deny at all costs or a remarkable ignorance and simplistic approach by the athletes. Both are probably highly prevalent.

7. Playing with the Big Boys

We have looked at the athletes along with their coaches and support teams but now it is time to scrutinise the national sports bodies, the high ranking officials and the judges who all play such a pivotal role in sport as a whole and the Olympic ideal.

Why should anyone wish to stage the Olympic Games? Some countries make a profit from hosting the Olympics, but this is not their prime motivation. Nowadays most make a loss, perhaps quite a substantial loss. There is much kudos around the Games and it is a chance to show off the nation and their attributes to the world. The Munich Games of 1936 was a classic example of using the Olympic stage for political ends but it was by no means the only one. The Moscow Olympics of 1980 and the Los Angeles Games of 1984 were both beset by political chicanery. The Americans boycotted the Moscow Olympics in protest at the invasion of Afghanistan, a cause that is not without irony. Margaret Thatcher wanted British athletes to join the boycott but unlike many national leaders she could not order them to do so. Many athletes snubbed her and went. It is said this may have been a positive factor in getting the Games to come to London in 2012, although between these dates the USA who had led the boycott hosted the Summer Games in Atlanta in 1996 and the Winter Games in Salt Lake City in 2002. Their boycott seems to have done them no harm. In 1984 when the Olympics were in Los Angeles the Soviet bloc had a tit-for-tat boycott of those games. The USA has hosted four Summer and four Winter Olympic Games, more than any other country in both categories.

NEW EVENTS

The Ancient Olympics started with just one event and finished with several. The modern Olympics started with a small number of events and has since grown to so many that it is widely believed that there are too many. Even the IOC wants to limit the growth. From time to time a new sport is introduced and rather less often another is removed. Many people will be surprised at which sports are in the Olympics and even more will be amazed at what used to be. Since the first modern Games in 1896 there are 10 sports that have disappeared completely. These are cricket, croquet, Jeu de Paume, lacrosse, motorboat racing, pelota, polo, roque, rackets and tug-of-war. Rugby was played in the Summer Olympics of 1900, 1908, 1920 and 1924. In 2016 in Brazil rugby sevens will make its debut and golf is due to return. Golf was an Olympic sport in 1900 and 1904. In 1900 there was a "Match de Cricket" in Paris between England and France. Most of the French team were British expatriates living in Paris. There are a number of events that have disappeared although the underlying sport remains. They include plunge for distance, underwater swimming, standing high jump (without a run up), tandem cycling and the shooting events of pigeon shooting (real not clay) and duelling pistol. In the last event the competitors did not shoot at each other but at a mannequin dressed in a frock coat with a Bull's eye on his throat.

Judo was introduced to the Games in 1964 when they were held in Tokyo. Taekwondo was introduced in 1988 when the Games were in Seoul in South Korea. Synchronised Swimming came in 1984 in Los Angeles. Beach Volleyball was first seen in 1996 in Atlanta. Olympic baseball first appeared in 1904 in St Louis and has been seen on and off since then. It became an official Olympic sport in 1992 but was omitted from London 2012. It seems in these cases that the host country was keen to introduce a new sport in which it had a strong chance of winning medals, preferably in gold. In London 2012 the new discipline of women's boxing was introduced and Great Britain won the first gold medal.

One of the criteria for being accepted as an Olympic sport is that it must be practiced by men in at least 75 countries on four continents, and by women in at least 40 countries on three continents. However, in some of these countries the sports would seem to have a tiny minority appeal. The choice of sports in the games is always controversial whether it is the very highly paid professional football, tennis and golf or the esoteric games.

HOSTING THE GAMES

For many of the countries who have held the games it has represented establishing themselves in the world order. In 1936 Germany was resurgent after the defeat of the First World War. It was also a political statement about Hitler's belief in the "master race". The Games were back in Munich in 1972 to show that Germany was back as a powerful democracy, at least in West Germany. The Tokyo Games in 1964 helped to show Japan as a rising economic power. The same is true of the Seoul Games in 1988 as South Korea had become the second largest economy in south-east Asia after Japan. At the time China was still recovering from the social and economic disaster of the Mao era. In 1992 Barcelona was restoring itself after years of fascism. General Franco died in 1975, in the year 1975 Spain had its first democratic elections since 1936 and Barcelona was discovering its identity as a Catalan state after years of its culture and language being suppressed. The Beijing Olympics in 2008 helped to establish China as a major world power and the 2016 Games in Rio are not just the first in South America (they were held in Mexico in 1968) but it emphasises the rising economic importance of Brazil as one of the BRIC nations. BRIC stands for Brazil, Russia, India and China and represents the four fastest growing of the large emerging economies.

The bidding process for hosting the Games starts years in advance. A bid has to show the International Olympic Committee (IOC) that the venue has the ability to deal with all the athletes and their entourages, the officials, the press and, of course, the many spectators. Infrastructure, including transport and accommodation must be good and much money is planned to be spend on new venues for events and an Olympic Village for the athletes. Security must be robust without being oppressive. A planned legacy after the Games is also required. If the IOC decides that a city has fulfilled the requirements it may be considered a "Candidate City" and it goes into the second phase of the process. The Candidate Cities for the 2016 Games were recognised in September 2007, nine years in advance. London was announced as the host city for 2012 in Singapore in July 2005, seven years in advance. The cost of commissioning such a proposal can be very significant but in addition there is an application fee to the IOC. For the 2012 Olympics this was US$150,000. The IOC makes a final judgment on which city is the best candidate for the coming Summer or Winter Olympic Games. There will be disappointed bidders. In 2005 Moscow, New York and Madrid were eliminated and in a two-way vote London beat Paris by 54 votes to 50. As there are 124 voting members this suggests that 20 abstained. London is the only city to have bid more than once and still hold a 100% record. Despite the time taken to scrutinise the bids a number of important facts seems to be have overlooked in the past. Did no one know about the incredibly poor air quality in Beijing in the summer? The bid for Atlanta Georgia gave an expected temperature of the mid-20s Celsius. This is the average temperature for day and night in July and August but on average the temperature will rise to over 30°C in the heat of the day. The IOC says that it is careful not to use political considerations but China had promised to clean up its act with regard to drugs in sport and to improve its record on human rights. As we have seen the clean-up of drugs seems to mean not getting caught rather than eliminating their use. Their record on human rights was no better.

The IOC officials have enormous power in their ability to vote for the successful applicant for the Games. It is a largely secret process but it has to be beyond reproach. Alas it seems that sportsmen and their coaches are not the only ones who may have scant regard for the rules.

Serious questions were asked about the probity of IOC officials when the truth emerged about the Salt Lake City bid to hold the 2002 Winter Games. Marc Hodler who was a long-standing member of the committee found clear evidence that up to 20 of the 110 members had been bribed to vote for Salt Lake City. There were many allegations included that the Salt Lake City organisers had paid for the family holidays of IOC members. Some had jobs or university places found for their relatives. The organisers paid for first-class travel and often gave lavish gifts. One member's wife received free cosmetic surgery. There are clear rules about the behaviour of IOC members when they visit potential host cities but these were widely ignored. An investigation followed and 13 members of the committee lost their positions. Nevertheless, it was claimed in 2004 that at least 70% of those who took gifts were still in the IOC.

Marc Hodler also alleged corruption over the course of 10 years in the selection of Atlanta, Nagano and Sydney. He explained that the losing cities did not complain because they may wish to bid again and so they did not want to make enemies within the system. Andrew Jennings wrote a book called "Lords of the Rings – Olympic Corruption". He said that Salt Lake City had the best bid for the 1998 Winter Games as so much was already present. They had a vast convention and press centre. There was already a 50,000-seat Olympic stadium. There was an Olympic village for 4,000 athletes and all the ski venues were in place. However, the Games were awarded to Nagano in Japan although it had far more work to do as facilities were poorly developed at the time. Rather than complaining, Salt Lake City decided to play the game and in a new and successful bid they gave "favours" with a total estimated value of between $3million and $7million.

Corruption went right to the top. In 2004 the South Korean IOC vice-president Kim Un-Yong was sentenced to two and a half years in prison for corruption. A court in South Korea convicted him of embezzling more than US$3million from sports organisations which he controlled as well as accepting $700,000 in bribes. It was a catastrophic end to the career of Kim Un-Yong who was a dominant figure in Korean sport for more than 30 years. He promoted Taekwondo overseas and helped it to become a full Olympic sport. He had helped in the successful bid for the Seoul Olympics in 1988, possibly with the aid of some bribes and he was implicated in the Salt Lake City scandal. The IOC executive board removed him from all his Olympic duties because of investigations by South Korean authorities and the IOC ethics commission. He was convicted of embezzling money whilst chairman of local and international Taekwondo federations. The court also found him guilty of accepting bribes from businessmen who wanted to serve on sports committees.

The problem did not go away. In 2004 reporters from the BBC programme *Panorama* posed as business consultants eager to bring the 2012 games Olympics to London. They approached freelance sports agents who claimed to have influence over certain IOC voters in exchange for a fee. At least one IOC member is thought to have agreed to meet the fake businessmen. The *Panorama* programme was criticised for rocking the boat shortly before the decision was made for the 2012 host nation. The four agents whom *Panorama* secretly filmed all had strong credentials in supporting successful bids. All claimed to be able to buy votes. Gabor Komyathy from Hungary claimed that he could ensure around 20 votes for London at a cost of 200,000 euros per vote. This comes to a total of €4million. Goran Takac from Serbia claimed that he could influence between 15 and 20 votes. He said that between seven and 10 of these votes would involve paying cash to IOC members. Mahmood el Farnawani from Egypt boasted that he could secure at least 14 votes by sticking to the rules but it would cost at least US$1.5million. Muttaleb Ahmed was a Kuwati who was the current director general of the Olympic Council of Asia. The organisation is responsible for running the Asian games and is partially funded by the IOC. Mr Ahmad was also involved in the Salt Lake City bid and was paid US$64,000 by them. He offered to set up meetings with 23 Asian members. He said that he did not pay people himself but *Panorama's* undercover company New London Ventures would have to do so. All four men come from countries in which bribery and corruption are endemic and a way of life.

The IOC Code of Ethics says that those involved in deciding an Olympic bid and their representatives are banned from soliciting, accepting or offering "any concealed remuneration, commission, benefit or service of any nature" related to the organisation of the Olympic games. Only gifts "of nominal value" may be given or accepted, and only as a sign of friendship, whatever that means. It adds that the parties "shall neither give nor accept instructions to vote or intervene in a given manner within the organs of the IOC". Cities involved in bidding "shall refrain ... from approaching another party, or third authority, with a view to obtaining any financial or political support inconsistent with the provisions" of the Code of Ethics.

Since 2004, at least three other IOC delegates have been expelled. One was a Bulgarian called Ivan Slavkov who was expelled in 2005 after being recorded offering the votes of colleagues. However, others, including the former French sports minister Guy Drut who was given a suspended prison sentence in 2005 for accepting payment for a fictitious job, remained in post.

Just before the opening of the 2012 Games the IOC had to consider a report from Swiss prosecutors about Joao Havelange who was a former president of FIFA, the governing body of world football. He had also been a member of the IOC. They found that in the 1990s he took multimillion-pound bribes linked to the World Cup. At the age of 94 he resigned from the IOC in December 2011 before its ethics committee was due to hold a hearing into the affair. The committee also had to investigate claims that 27 Olympic national committee officials and agents broke rules about ticket sales for the London Games. In some cases they offered tickets for re-sale at 10 times their face value.

There was an absence of adequate leadership from the top. Too often the leaders ran the IOC as their private domain, ignoring the problems of drugs in sport and corruption of officials. They preferred not to know. From 1980 to 2001 the IOC was led by Juan Antonio Samaranch. He was

Spanish and the First Marquis of Samarach. He was a former fascist and member of General Franco's government. He insisted on being addressed as "Your Excellency". He did manage to guide the movement from the edge of bankruptcy to a very healthy bank balance but he was often criticised for excessive commercialisation and sponsorship in sport. His rule was one of autocracy and blindness to the blatant problems within the organisation but he was by no means unique as a president of the IOC with these qualities. The IOC is not the only organisation to be accused of being oblivious to its problems and run by autocrats. There are plenty of criticisms of FIFA, the world governing body of football. Jacques Rogge was elected as IOC president in 2001 and promised to end corruption in the movement. He is a Belgian who graduated in medicine in Ghent and worked as an orthopaedic surgeon. He represented Belgium in yachting in the 1968, 1972 and 1976 Olympics and also represented his country at rugby, a sport for which Belgium is not renowned. As a doctor and sports physician he had no excuse for failure to understand the problems of doping.

Under his leadership the IOC has established links with Interpol and various money-laundering agencies and it set up an anti-corruption monitoring company. He tried to strengthen the judging and refereeing rules. One of his first challenges was at the Salt Lake City Winter Olympics in his first year in office. A French figure-skating judge was involved in vote-swapping with a Russian judge in the ice dance competition. He personally overturned the result and he has since forced international federations to change rules in skating, boxing, gymnastics, fencing, Taekwondo and wrestling to make them more objective. In 2010 he urged Sepp Blatter, the president of FIFA to clean up football and to do with it what he had done with the IOC. The reluctance of FIFA to accept technology to see if the ball has crossed the goalline is typical of the antiquated attitude but problems run much deeper.

BOYCOTTING THE GAMES

The USA and their friends including West Germany and Japan but not Great Britain boycotted the Moscow Olympics in 1980. The USSR and their friends had a boycott of Los Angeles in 1984. As has been mentioned already the first boycott was in response to the Soviet invasion of Afghanistan and the second was a tit for tat. There were 14 countries in the latter boycott but this was the year that the People's Republic of China chose to return to the Olympic fold. The Olympics is supposed to be above politics but these incidents are by no means isolated. The Olympic Charter calls on all countries to "resist all pressures of any kind whatsoever, whether of a political, religious or economic nature". Like so many other rules it is often ignored.

At the 1956 Games in Melbourne there was a boycott by Lichtenstein, the Netherlands, Spain, and Sweden in protest of the Soviet invasion of Hungary. At the same time Egypt, Lebanon and Iraq boycotted because of the Suez crisis. The People's Republic of China refused to participate as Taiwan was included as "the Republic of China".

Between 1964 and 1992 South Africa was banned because of apartheid.

At the 1976 Games in Montreal there was a boycott by 26 African countries in protest at New Zealand's participation. Earlier that year the New Zealand All Blacks rugby team had undertaken a three-month tour of South Africa but the IOC refused to ban them. Egypt competed for the first three days of the Games before withdrawing in support of the boycott by most other African nations. In addition, Taiwan as "The Republic of China" was barred from entering Canada, but then allowed to enter and compete if they agreed to change their name. The authorities in Taiwan considered this unacceptable and withdrew.

In 1988 the Games were in Seoul in South Korea. North Korea, which was still technically at war with the South, initially wanted to be joint hosts but when this was refused they boycotted the Games instead. Cuba and Ethiopia joined them in solidarity but there were no widespread boycotts for the first time since 1972.

Barcelona in 1992 was a landmark. There were no boycotts. The USSR had broken up and the constituent countries competed individually. South Africa returned to the fold and after the fall of the Berlin Wall Germany competed as a united country.

There was talk of a boycott of the Beijing Olympic Games in 2008 in response to China's treatment of Tibet and other human rights abuses but no major protest occurred.

London 2012 was free of boycott but there were calls to boycott the 2014 Winter Games in Sochi because of President Putin's oppression of homosexuals.

OBJECTIVE ASSESSMENTS

In some sports such as gymnastics, diving, figure skating and even boxing the award of marks can be very subjective and at times the marks seem so unexpected that there is suspicion of foul play. Was the judge biased or bribed? Sometimes, where there are several judges, the highest and the lowest marks are ignored and only the rest are summated. Removing the more extreme marks aims to resolve bias where it occurs.

Some of the judging in the Taekwondo in the 2008 Olympics in Beijing can be regarded as bizarre or grossly incompetent at best. This, along with the abominable behaviour of the Cuban Angel Matos and his coach should have been enough to have Taekwondo suspended from the Olympics until they had proved that they had their house in order.

At the 1988 Games in Seoul, in the final of the welterweight division an American boxer called Roy Jones Jr fought South Korea's Park Si-hun. Neutral commentators said that the American dominated the fight, landing more than two punches for every one received. Most observers thought he was the clear winner but the judges disagreed. They gave the gold medal to the Korean. Years later an investigator found a report in the archives of the Stasi, the disbanded East German secret police, by Karl-Heinz Wehr who was a Stasi agent and a former general secretary of the International Amateur Boxing Federation. Wehr said that a Korean millionaire had bribed senior boxing federation officials to rig fights in favour of Koreans. Hiouad Larbi, a Moroccan judge in the Jones fight, admitted to newspaper reporters that he had falsified his scorecard.

In the words of the Roman Poet Juvenal, "quis custodiet ipsos custodes?" or "Who will guard the guards?" How can we expect athletes to behave when there is so much corruption in the hierarchy of sport? The leaders must lead by example.

MATCH FIXING

It is not only corruption and bribery of judges and officials that leads to fraudulent results. Sometimes the sportsmen are corrupt and lose intentionally. With the exception of cases such as badminton players intentionally losing matches to gain a better draw in the next round or a runner dropping out of the 800 metres to concentrate on the 1,500 metres final, I am unable to find evidence of Olympic athletes losing intentionally and passing up the glory. This may be because it is such a prestigious event that occurs only once every four years and because there is no direct financial reward. Where there are cases of sportsmen deliberately losing matches to their disadvantage, there always seems to be a very heavy culture of betting that accompanies it. The Olympics does not seem to attract a great deal of betting.

One of the most notorious examples of corruption is said to be the "throwing" of the World Series in 1919. For those not familiar, the World Series is the American national baseball championship and it does not contain a single team from outside the USA. The fact that they call it the World Series rather than the US National says much about how the Americans view the world. Joseph Jefferson Jackson, known as "Shoeless Joe" was alleged to be the ringleader of this scandal. He and seven teammates from the Chicago White Sox were accused of conspiring with gamblers to lose the final of the 1919 World Series to the Cincinnati Reds. They faced a trial in 1921 but a jury acquitted them. However, the newly appointed baseball commissioner Judge Kenesaw Mountain Landis barred them for life from professional baseball. The extent to which "Shoeless Joe" was involved is controversial.

He claimed that his teammates had given his name to the gamblers although he had not agreed to participate. The other players admitted that he had not attended meetings about fixing the match. In 1920 Jackson signed a confession stating that he was paid $5,000 although he had been offered $20,000. Later he claimed that a team lawyer had manipulated him into signing the document which he had failed to understand. Jackson was illiterate. He never learned to read or write but he was a national hero. He also said that he had tried to talk about the plan to Charles Comiskey, the owner of the White Sox both before and after the series but he was rebuffed. We may wonder why Charles Comiskey was so impervious to such an allegation.

Was Shoeless Joe Jackson a simple man who had been corrupted or a scapegoat for the sins of others? A ringleader who never attended the meetings where important decisions were made seems unlikely. His performance that day suggests that if he intended to throw the match he was remarkably incompetent at it. He made no errors and scored 12 hits which stood as a World Series record until 1964. If he was trying to throw the game he was making a remarkably bad job of it.

In snooker Stephen Lee was given a 12 years ban for match fixing in 2013. Snooker may be seen as a pastime rather than a sport. This was by no means the only allegation of match fixing in snooker and the list of allegations and convictions is quite substantial. Snooker, football and cricket appear to be the most susceptible to match fixing as a result of betting. Ladbroke's is a very large British bookmaking company. It is said to be a tenth of the size of the Hong Kong Jockey Club in terms of gambling turnover and this is just one tenth of the size of illegal betting in China.

Throughout the world football has had many cases of match fixing and spot fixing. Not all betting in football is over the big matches. In 2013 there was concern about the volume of betting in Asia on matches in the Conference South League, especially those involving Billericay, Hornchurch and Chelmsford. Although there did not seem to be any evidence of connivance from these modest teams it did seem amazing that they should interest Asian gamblers and that the Football Association should have done so little to investigate. However, the police did investigate and a number of arrests followed. There is a great deal of interest in English football from Asian gamblers but it is suggested that this is because it is so difficult to corrupt. The lower leagues are easier to fix. A bribe of perhaps £10,000 may be a great deal of money to someone from a lower league. In the Premiership that may not represent even one day's pay or even one day's pay after tax. Perhaps it is the vast amount that they get paid that makes them relatively immune from match fixing. However, even the well paid footballers can get into trouble with an injudicious betting habit of their own. They are unable to abuse drugs as they get tested. They are unable to abuse alcohol as it would impede their training. Gambling is their vice.

SPOT FIXING

We use the term "it's just not cricket" to describe anything that seems unfair but cricket is a sport that has suffered considerable from match fixing. It is subject to very heavy betting on the Indian subcontinent and that is where most of the trouble has occurred. Betting is not limited to the final result of a match but to such random matters as when a no-ball may be bowled or how many runs may be scored in a particular over. This is called spot fixing. A list of 16 cricketers who have been banned from test or one-day international matches includes five from India, five from Pakistan, one from Bangladesh, three from South Africa, one from the West Indies and one from Kenya. However, it would be wrong to assume that British sportsmen do not do that sort of thing. Mervyn Westfield of Essex was banned for five years for spot fixing in 2010 but his career ended in 2012 when he was imprisoned for the offence. Danish Kaneria, also of Essex was also implicated and given a life ban. The latter was a Pakistani player who played in the English county game for Essex but Mervyn Westfield was educated in England.

Football is also susceptible to spot fixing. An example of the latter may be putting the ball out for a corner-kick at a specified time. However, there have been confessions of spot fixing in English football, even at a high level and the FA should show due concern.

Many players who would baulk at losing a game intentionally do not see a great moral problem in spot fixing as it does not usually affect the outcome of the match. It is dishonest and it involves playing into the hands of some of the most despicable elements of society. It is corrupt and illegal.

It is not just the vast rewards that are open to some sportsmen that tempt them to cheat. When a great deal of money rests on an outcome in sport, whether it is who gets to host a games or the results of gambling, there will be a temptation to some to succumb to bribery as the sums offered may seem quite substantial for so little. This requires vigilance and discipline from the sport backed by criminal charges if appropriate.

8. Sports products

"Inspire a generation" was the clarion call of the 2012 London Olympics and we were inspired. It is not just serious athletes who participate in sports but sport for all. Increased physical activity throughout the nation is to be encouraged. Obesity is an enormous problem and a contributor to many premature deaths from heart disease, stroke, diabetes and cancer. The World Health Organisation states that obesity is second only to smoking as an avoidable cause of cancer in the western world. Even for those who are not obese, indolence is a strong risk factor for disease. For those who are obese, physical activity appears to reduce their risk. Physical activity in later life may even help to ward off dementia. A survey of adults found that British women were the most obese in Europe whilst British men were second behind the Maltese. German men came 10th and German women were outside the top ten. Nowadays obesity in childhood is so common that many parents fail to recognise it. The situation is getting worse. We should all try to take regular exercise. Many have been inspired and there is a market out there waiting to offer us equipment, sports drinks, healthy foods and nutritional supplements.

Much is marketed as being scientifically based when it is not. As we have seen, there is a great deal of science behind top athletic performance when it comes to getting away with taking performance enhancing drugs. However, much else to do with training and coaching is far less evidence based than we may assume. A search of the scientific literature to find the best method of training is mostly unrewarding. Often where research exists it is of poor quality. Even such fundamentals as the benefit of warming up before exercise are not well documented by high quality research. That is not to suggest that it should be scrapped.

It may well be useful and it seems unlikely to do harm but it has not been put to the vigorous test. Diet, vitamins and other supplements are governed more by folklore and the dictum of self-appointed gurus than by well researched evidence. Proper randomised controlled trials with an adequate number of participants are a rarity and in reality we may not be as far on from the days when smoking was advocated to increase lung volume and strychnine was given to help endurance as we may like to believe. What is promoted to the general public often seems to imply a strong scientific base but this is usually lacking.

At the time of the London Olympics the *BMJ*, formerly the *British Medical Journal* printed a series of articles that condemned many practices as having little or no scientific validity and being the result of self-serving marketing ploys. This applied especially to the field of sports drinks which are now the fastest growing area of the soft drinks market. However, the problem is much more extensive than this.

When we want to train the first thing we need is some basic kit. Preposterous prices are charged for football shirts to show allegiance to a specific team, even in children's sizes. The *BMJ* articles were very unenthusiastic about trainers but as one who remembers running cross country at school in plimsolls, I regard them as a great advance. However, not all the supposed high tech is as sound or as necessary as the manufacturers would like us to believe. A good cushion sole protects the lower limb from the repeated trauma of running, especially on a hard surface but the value of gels in compartments that can be punctured by a thorn if running outside or air cushions is less obvious. The quality of the finished product is highly variable and price may be a poor guide except that the cheapest are almost invariably shoddy. They are not carefully crafted by skilled technicians but usually assembled in third world countries in dimly lit workshops by people who work excessive hours for a pittance of pay. These workers might also be children. Avoid leather uppers in trainers as they let the feet get too hot and increase the risk of fungal infection. A loose weave is preferable. Ask yourself what you need from trainers and if those shoes give it to you.

There is debate about how they affect running style and whether we should be running heel-toe or running on our toes. Shoes with a high heel leading to heel-toe running may put grater strain on the knees. Some people have advocated minimalist shoes that are basically just four millimetres of rubber but they have been associated with more injuries. There is debate about the correct degree of support and the desirability of the heel tab. However, all in all I regard trainers as one of the better sports products.

SPORTS DRINKS AND HYDRATION

Nowadays a great deal of attention is paid to adequate hydration during training and competition. Dehydration does have an adverse effect on performance. When I was at school, players in rugby matches were given a segment of orange at half time to replace lost fluids. That was a pathetic token but matters have gone too far the other way. When I see joggers out on a Sunday morning, clutching a water bottle in their hand, I wonder how far and how fast they are going and how much their performance would be poorer without it. This is not sports science. This is an affectation, but it does sell plastic water bottles. Many schools in the UK now encourage children to stop every 15 to 20 minutes during exercise to drink. This is based on supposedly expert advice but it was written by people with financial links to the sports drinks industry and it does not stand up to scrutiny. In fact, having to stop every 15 to 20 minutes for a drink is quite ridiculous. Football teams instruct children to bring a bottle and no football field is complete without a colourful array of sports drinks rather than water from the tap. Many of the bottles are left behind as the children have not been instructed about clearing up after themselves.

Much supposedly expert advice comes from people who are employed by the manufacturers of sports drinks and is based on bad science. The value of sports drinks in the UK alone is thought to be around £260 million a year and growing. The science is often seriously flawed but not the marketing.

Endurance events such as the marathon have ample drinking stations where those who feel thirsty may drink. If we are truly dehydrated we feel thirsty and no athlete with access to water will become dehydrated. The articles in the *BMJ* were very clear about this. Over-hydration in endurance events is a much more common problem than under-hydration. Taking in too much water reduces the blood sodium level and this is far more dangerous. Symptoms include changes in mental function from mild withdrawal to confusion and possibly seizures and coma. Furthermore, athletes with this condition may have persistent thirst and so continue to drink, thereby aggravating the condition. After a marathon many more people need treatment for over-hydration than under-hydration. This is especially true of those who are not very good runners as they spend more hours on the course expending fewer calories per hour and so sweating less. There have been 16 recorded deaths and 1,600 people taken critically ill during competitive marathon running due to a drop in their blood sodium; in other words over-hydration. There is no evidence that anyone doing a modern marathon has ever died of dehydration. Nevertheless, it is dehydration that gets the attention because this is where the market lies. Advertisers have managed to create a new "disease" of dehydration when it is not really a problem. They have declared that athletes should drink as much as is tolerable. They advise that thirst is not a reliable guide to dehydration. The authors in the *BMJ* strongly disagree. No one mentions the serious problem of over-hydration. The companies that produce the products have managed to get their appointees and employees on to expert committees so that their message has come across as the official stance. Sports teams and individuals have started to blame dehydration rather than poor training or inadequate preparation for defeats as if to say, "If only we had drunk more of this sports drink we would have won." Sports bodies receive generous funding from the industry and they repay.

There are a number of types of fault in the evidence. Sometimes the scientific evidence is nothing like as strong as is implied. On other occasions it does apply to elite athletes in serious training but that does not mean that it can be extrapolated to the rest of us mere mortals who are trying to keep fit and keep our weight down. One of the articles in the *BMJ* states, "Over the past 40 years humans have been misled—mainly by the marketing departments of companies selling sports drinks—to believe that they need to drink to stay ahead of thirst to be optimally hydrated. In fact, relatively small increases in total body water can be fatal. A two percent increase in total body water produces generalised oedema (swelling) that can impair athletic and mental performance; greater levels of overhydration result in hyponatraemic encephalopathy (disease of the brain from low sodium) – severe cerebral oedema (swelling of the brain) that produces confusion, seizures, coma, and ultimately death from respiratory arrest." The parentheses are mine to explain the medical terms in the simplest way.

If the danger is from hyponatraemia or low blood sodium rather than dehydration, should we take salt in our fluids whilst exercising or should we just drink less? When we sweat we lose mostly water but some salt too. The sweat glands are very good at removing salt from the fluid they secrete but if the rate of sweating increases they become less effective. Hence, the more sweat that is produced the higher the concentration of salt in it. Thus, increasing the sweat rate three-fold may increase salt loss ten-fold. However, acclimatisation to heat leads to more efficient sweating so that for a given rate of sweating less salt is lost. There are reserves of salt in the bones and the kidneys will retain salt if there is a shortage. Hence it would seem that the better approach is to drink less rather than to take extra salt that may also be very unpalatable and cause nausea. However, if heavy exercise is anticipated in very hot conditions, especially if the person is not acclimatised, some extra salt may be of value, probably with meals rather than in drink. For the ordinary person this is not required and impartial expert advice is that we should keep salt intake low to reduce the risk of developing high blood pressure. There does not appear to be any significant advantage in having drinks with salt in them and sports drinks are no less likely to lead to low sodium or hyponatraemia than plain water. We should just drink less and be guided by thirst.

I sometimes see people exercising whilst wearing an excessive amount of clothing for the conditions. Some wear what looks like a plastic track suit and these are called sweat suits. On occasions when I have asked them, they have told me that they are trying to lose weight. I find this astounding. Sweat suits are commercially available and advertised to help with weight loss. If the person was to weigh himself before and after such exercise then sweating profusely would lead to weight loss provided that he did not drink. The weight loss is water loss. He will be dehydrated and thirsty. Therefore he will drink. His kidneys will retain water and the weight will go back on. What they really want to lose is fat. We sweat water and a small amount of salt. We do not sweat fat. We do not sweat calories. If we exercise hard we sweat. If we exercise harder we sweat more because we are using more Calories and have to lose more heat. That does not mean that simply sweating more without doing any more exercise will increase the rate of burning Calories.

An Internet search found a large number of organisations that sell sweat suits and many testimonials as to how good they are. Testimonials are not scientific evidence. They are selected plaudits, ignoring all criticism and they are a total waste of time. In fairness, there are also many people on the Internet who point out that this is an illusion. It is not only the stupid who are gullible. I once found the London University captain of judo training with a track suit beneath his judo suit on a hot evening in July. He told me that he was trying to lose weight and I explained why this was a fallacy. He rapidly understood the science, as I would have expected from a person doing a PhD in physics.

Sweat suits are designed to cause dehydration. If they prevent heat loss by evaporation of sweat they may also cause heat stroke. Heat stroke is not normally caused by dehydration and nor is collapse. It is the result of the body temperature rising. Heat stroke is produced by vigorous exercise in a hot environment and is not more likely in those who are dehydrated. Collapse is usually because blood vessels are open and the blood pressure drops. Lying down to recover is perfectly adequate and massive fluid intake is not required or desirable.

Marketing is organised by people with a product to sell and plastic bottles to hold ordinary tap water have a limited volume of sales. The market for sports drinks is enormous. That is not to suggest that imaginative marketing of water does not occur. We all have access to safe drinking water from the tap but the market for bottled water is worth many millions of pounds a year. The fact that it is possible to buy bottled water at 75p a pint and bottled milk at 25p a pint shows how much the market and the consumer's common sense may be distorted. However, even that does not match the marketing of water under the name of homeopathy. Now is not the place to discuss homeopathy but basically the practitioner spends about an hour with the patient to be able to personalise the treatment and then gives a bottle of tap water to take away.

Fluid is not absorbed directly from the stomach to any significant extent and for water or other nutrients to be absorbed they have to empty into the small intestine. Plain water will empty fairly quickly. Proteins and more especially fat will slow the rate of stomach emptying considerably. This is the rationale for having something fatty to eat before embarking on a night of drinking. It is not to coat the stomach to prevent alcohol from being absorbed directly into the circulation. No significant absorption occurs directly from the stomach. A very small amount of dissolved salt and sugar may cause the fluid to empty faster from the stomach than plain water. This is called an isotonic solution as the concentration is the same as in the blood. Hence, sports drinks are advertised as being isotonic. However, whether this is practically important is rather dubious. Sometimes advertisements suggest that their product will rehydrate faster after exercise. This may be true but it does not matter. There is no great urgency after the exercise is over. More concentrated drinks would empty from the stomach more slowly and are not to be recommended. This applies particularly to drinks that are high in sugar. The value of the Calories present in sports drinks or other drinks in an endurance event such as the marathon is rather dubious. Eating plenty of carbohydrate the night before is much more important. The value of glucose during exercise is an example of bad and biased science as some of the research was based on people who had been starved before exertion. This is not a normal situation in sport.

The international system of units that scientists use are called SI units and the unit for energy is the joule, abbreviated to j. However, in nutrition calories are often used. One calorie is the energy required to raise one gram of water from 14.5 to 15.5°C. This is equivalent to 4.16 joules. However, the calorie is a rather small unit and so kilocalories or kcal are usually used. They may also be called Calories or Cal with a capital C. It is a very common error to write energy requirements with a small c when a capital is required. In this section Calories will be used to imply kilocalories.

In the world of advertising, something that is low in Calories is "slimming" whilst something that is high in Calories "gives you energy". This means "contains lots of Calories" and it would be more accurate to say "makes you fat". For a great many of us who are not elite athletes or serious club athletes, a major benefit from exercise is to lose weight or to try to prevent us from getting fat. It is a simple balance between Calories consumed and Calories expended that determines whether we gain weight, lose weight or stay the same. Therefore, if we are out exercising to lose weight and taking in Calories, it will undo at least some of the benefit which we are hoping to obtain. Sports drinks do not normally contain any fat or protein but they do have carbohydrate, mostly in the form of sugars, and carbohydrate gives 410 Calories per 100 grams. As a comparison, protein gives about the same whilst 100 grams of fat yields 930 Calories and 100 grams of alcohol contains 700 Calories.

The following table gives an indication of the amount of carbohydrate (abbreviated to carbs), sugar, Calories and salt in a number of the more popular sports drinks. All are per 500ml. The number of Calories sometimes seems to be less than expected from the total amount of carbohydrate. This is because some may be as soluble fibre that is not absorbed and so will not produce Calories. The figures are from the manufacturers' websites. Isostar is not included as its manufacturer is rather coy about its sugar, Calories and salt content. The volume consumed during a training session will depend upon the individual but it may rather more than 500ml and closer to a litre or more.

PRODUCT	CARBS	SUGAR	SALT	CALORIES
Lucozade Sports Lite	10	2.5	trace	20.5
Lucozade Sport Body Fuel	32	17.5	trace	140
Lucozade Energy	86	86	trace	350
Lucozade Revive	15	14.5	trace	65
Gatorade	30	30	2.5 grams	125
Powerade ION4	19.5	19.5	0.5 grams	85

This shows that whilst the Calorie intake is unlikely to exceed the Calories used in the exercise, it may have been better to have drunk plain water instead. Lucozade Sports Lite is far lower in Calories than most sports drinks whilst Lucozade Energy, which is promoted as a sports drink, is basically the old fashioned Lucozade with a lot of sugar. With the exception of Gatorade, the amount of salt is small. A litre of Gatorade would provide 5 grams of salt which is close to the maximum daily recommended daily intake of 6 grams.

There is often an implication on the websites that taking sugar during exercise prevents the blood glucose level from falling too far. This is not said overtly but it is certainly implied. This is nonsense. Diabetics try hard to prevent their blood glucose from getting too high as there is strong evidence that this is linked to complications including coronary heart disease and stroke. If a diabetic takes too much insulin and blood glucose falls too far there will be confusion, incoordination, aggression, slurred speech and if it falls far enough there may be convulsions and even death. However, those of us who do not take insulin do not have that risk. The body has a system involving insulin and glucagon which keeps blood glucose within a normal range. People who do not take insulin who exercise even to exhaustion do not have blood glucose below a normal fasting level. High blood sugar does not confer any advantage such as getting glucose into the muscles more readily. Glucose is actively absorbed into muscles with the help of insulin and exercise improves the sensitivity to insulin.

The alleged need to keep hydrated has gone beyond sports training and many young people now walk the streets with a bottle in their hand. This may be worse than just an affectation as they may be drinking a beverage that is high in sugar and high in Calories, leading to obesity as well as tooth decay. There is a myth that a mixture of sugar and caffeine gives energy. It is empty Calories. As a single scientific paper is of limited value I have looked for systematic reviews that consider the validity of many papers and eventually form a conclusion based on much evidence. Both glucose and caffeine increase endurance slightly but together there is no additional benefit. A review of studies shows that the two together actually produce a slightly worse performance than either alone. All the studies are based on trained athletes in high intensity performance. None looks at ordinary teenagers walking the streets and asks if a bottle of fizzy sugar solution with caffeine gives them energy or just makes them fat. Cola contains phosphoric acid that can dissolve tooth enamel. Try taking a dirty old copper coin and leave it soaked in a saucer of cola overnight. In the morning the coin will be gleaming. Imagine what that does to your teeth.

The following table examines the sugar, caffeine and Calories per 500ml in some of the more popular sugary drinks. Again the data is derived from their websites. Sometimes it has been extrapolated from 330ml cans to 500ml sizes. A cup of instant coffee will give about 100mg of caffeine. Caffeine is in milligrams, carbohydrate in grams.

PRODUCT	CARBS	CAFFEINE	CALORIES
Coca-Cola	53	48	210
Coca-Cola cherry	56	48	226
Glaceau vitamin water orange	23	71	100
Red Bull Energy Drink	55	80	225
Dr Pepper	51.7	59	210

All products can be obtained in a sugar free form and only one variation of Glaceau vitamin drink contains caffeine. The Lucozade Brands are owned by the enormous pharmaceutical firm Glaxo Smith Klein (GSK) whilst Powerade, Glaceau and Dr Pepper are produced by the Coca Cola Company. Gatorade is owned by Pepsi Cola. Coca Cola is a sponsor of the London Olympics and has been an important contributor to Olympics for many years. GSK is a service provider. People who drink two litres a day of sugar-containing Coca Cola, Red Bull or Dr Pepper are taking in nearly a thousand Calories a day of surplus energy. This does not mean that they are full of vitality and "bursting with energy". It means that they are in danger of getting very fat very fast.

The marketing of such product as "sports drinks" or "energy drinks" is very clever as it can give the impression that the person is looking after his body and even improving his fitness without even breaking into a sweat. In fact he is taking in sugar and taking in Calories and he will probably eat just as much for his next meal. Fast sugar is bad. It may well be more important than fat in causing obesity and heart disease.

A team from University College London reported on findings from a dental clinic set up to treat sportsmen and women at the 2012 Olympics. They found a considerable amount of tooth and gum disease in a group that may be expected to be in excellent general health. Their dental health was not comparable with their other physical health. Although it was not possible to make a definitive statement about the cause of this poor dental health a likely candidate is taking a lot of sugary drinks. We know that sugar in drinks is bad for teeth. It seems reasonable to suggest that sports drinks are rotting their teeth and the athletes would do better with plain water.

Lucozade Lite™ is advertised as "fitness hydration". It does help hydration as it contains water. So does the stuff from the tap. Fitness you have to achieve yourself. Simply drinking the product will not make you fit.

Conducting a large clinical trial is not easy and not cheap but it is the only way to test these products. Hence researchers are eager to take finance from people who stand to profit by a positive result. This can be a problem in drug trials and nowadays medical journals like to know and to publish the fact if the research or any of the researchers was funded by a body with a vested interest. There is pressure from the funders to present results in the most positive light. There is pressure not to publish negative findings. Basically, he who pays the piper calls the tune. That is not to say that all research funded by those with a vested interest is bad or fraudulent. However, it should be viewed with a degree of circumspection. This is particularly the case when expert guidance is written by people who are employed or funded by the sports drinks industry. The pharmaceutical industry often sponsors research into drugs, but they do not normally get to write the expert advice.

A well conducted scientific trial should involve a fairly large number of participants. About half are randomly allocated to receive the substance under trial, such as the sports drink and the rest receive the control which may be plain water. Ideally it should be disguised so that neither group knows which they are receiving. This is obviously difficult with water versus sports drink as they taste different but one may contain sugar and the other an artificial sweetener. If it is a single event such as a marathon race, it is important that the people in the test group and the control groups are similar. If it is a time trial it may be possible to run it twice and on each occasion the person has either the test or the control drink. Hence they act as their own control. Ideally they should not know which they have taken each time. These are called randomised controlled trials.

The trials that have been used to assess sports drinks have often used too few people to have a good chance of really showing significance. If they are a fairly narrow group such as highly trained cyclists it is not necessary to have as many as if they are a diverse group such as middle aged men and women who are trying to keep fit. In a review of 106 studies of marathon runners, there was one study with 257 runners and this was the only with more than 100 subjects. For small group studies, 100 subjects is generally regarded as the smallest acceptable size. The next largest study was 54 subjects and the median size was nine. Median means that half the studies had nine or more subjects and half had nine or fewer. In other words, most of the 106 studies were not just small but tiny and so were unreliable.

It is important to be measuring something that is both relevant and important. Many studies used time to exhaustion or other outcomes that are not directly relevant to performance in real life events. One study used time to exhaustion after 75 minutes of preliminary exercise. It found an improvement of 33% in the time to exhaustion after the 75 minutes had been completed. The 75 minutes should have been included and this would have reduced the improvement to just three percent. Biological outcomes do not necessarily correlate with improved performance. Reductions in use of muscle glycogen, for example, did not correlate with improved athletic performance. Glycogen is how glucose is stored in muscle. Physiological outcomes such as maximal oxygen consumption have also been shown to be poor predictors of performance, even among elite athletes.

Another problem is that results have been based on highly trained athletes and then assumed to be just as applicable to the ordinary population. This is not valid.

With many small trials there is a tendency for only the positive ones to get published but the negative ones are just as important. It is as important to know what does not work as what does. If someone looks at the literature as a whole and tries to draw a conclusion he may be misled by being presented with only the trials that gave positive results. Many of the people on the editorial board of sports medicine journals are in the pay of the sports drinks industry and so they may be reluctant to publish papers that are not in the interest of their paymasters and rather too eager to publish those that are. The industry has funded hundreds of such trials. It is easy to pick and choose what to publish.

A team at the Centre of Evidence Based Medicine at Oxford University assessed the evidence behind 431 performance enhancing claims in advertisements for 104 different sports products including sports drinks, protein shakes and trainers. Only three (2.7%) of the studies were judged to be of high quality and at low risk of bias. They say this absence of high quality evidence is "worrying" and call for better research in this area to help inform decisions.

PROTEIN SHAKES AND SUPPLEMENTS

We all need protein in our diet and people who are in intense training have an increased need. The British Nutrition Foundation is a scientific and educational charity that promotes evidence-based nutritional knowledge and advice. It is highly respected and its views are quoted by the NHS "Choices" website. It says that men aged 19 to 50 need about 55.5 grams of protein a day whilst women of that age need around 45 grams. The average daily intake of 88 grams a day for men and 64 grams a day for women suggests that very few of us eat a diet that is deficient in protein. Those involved in serious training need more protein and the Foundation suggests that endurance athletes require between 1.2 and 1.4g per kg of body weight daily, while those competing in strength and speed events need between 1.2 and 1.7g per kg of body weight. Even for a person of 100kg eating 1.7 grams per kilogram, that is less than half a pound of lean meat a day. In September 2010 the British Nutritional Foundation stated that "We would generally not recommend protein shakes for athletes or people doing exercise as the body's protein needs can be met through a healthy varied diet."

Research from 2010 by the US organization *"Consumer Reports"* (rather similar to our *Which?)* looked at 15 protein powders and found that some protein drinks were contaminated with heavy metals such as arsenic, cadmium, lead and mercury. They explained that there are small amounts of heavy metals in the environment and it will find its way into food but three products raised "particular concern" because consuming three servings a day could produce a daily exposure that exceeded recommended limits of arsenic, cadmium and lead. Cadmium accumulates in the kidneys and can cause damage to them. It can also damage the liver and may cause cancer. The toxicity of lead and arsenic is well known and arsenic may also cause cancer.

We eat protein in food and this is broken down to its constituent amino acids which can be re-used to form more protein and what is not used is metabolized to give Calories. Protein gives 410 Calories per 100 grams, the same as carbohydrate. Protein is sometimes classified as first or second class according to how good it is at providing the required amino acids to make muscle. By and large, animal protein such as meat, fish and dairy products is first class whilst vegetable protein is second class. Some amino acids can be synthesized in the body from others. Some cannot and must be taken in the diet. They are called essential amino acids.

Hence to build a kilogram of muscle will require more than a kilogram of protein in the diet but not a vast amount more. It is unlikely that the limiting factor in terms of speed of building muscle is a shortage of protein in the diet, even for a vegetarian. Many competitors in the power events such as shot put and discus, as well as strong man competitions are actually obese. They eat a considerable amount of protein each day and even lean meat has fat. They often have a very unhealthy physique with a high cholesterol and risk of diabetes. A kilogram of protein that is not used to build more protein gives 4,100 Calories. If a person who indulges in a power sport is dieting to lose weight he may possibly find a slight loss of power unless he increases his protein consumption a little. Otherwise, a normal weight loss diet is fine.

All the protein that is required can be obtained from a balanced diet. There is plenty of protein in meat, fish, dairy produce, eggs but also in bread and potatoes. Nevertheless, it is common to find that gyms, sporting goods outlets, "health food shops" and even pharmacies sell protein supplements and protein shakes. The protein sold is often whey protein from milk. The vendors claim that it contains the right amino acids in the right ratio for body building. As we have seen, this is nonsense and a good diet is all that is required. I looked at the whey protein for sale in my own gym and found that 2.25 kilograms costs £42. This is a considerable price for something that is basically the waste product from cheese manufacture. I said that the best fillet steak would be cheaper than that and probably a lot nicer. The gym manager was honest enough to say that it would probably be better for me too but they sold those products because there is a demand. It is also possible to buy a protein shake after training. Presumably the idea here is that after exercise this protein will then go straight to making more muscle. Are people really this gullible? There is a limit to how fast it is possible to gain muscle, even with vigorous exercise and a good diet but for most of us it is not an inadequate supply of protein in the diet that will be the limiting factor and so there is no advantage to taking more protein.

I was pleased when I noticed an advertisement in the gym from a local butcher as good meat is preferable to protein supplements. However, I was perplexed when I noticed that he advertised lean steak burgers that had "0% carbs." This begs two questions. The first is why should I want a carbohydrate free burger? Carbohydrates provide glucose, the basic substance of energy. The second is how do they get meat carbohydrate free? Muscle stores glucose as glycogen. Therefore it contains carbohydrate. Do they exercise the cattle to exhaustion to deplete all glycogen before slaughter? That would not go down well with the animal welfare groups.

There is a conflict between the altruism of demanding scientific evidence and the commercial demand of selling nonsense which customers want and will pay for. We may hope that gyms would be offering a more scientific approach but even more so may we expect it from pharmacies. I found whey supplements for sale in my local Asda pharmacy but even that is nothing besides my local Cooperative pharmacy that sells magnets that are supposed to have therapeutic properties. They are on sale because people actually buy them. They are on sale at places that people may think they can trust. This trust is betrayed by selling these nonsensical products.

There is often a tendency to believe that because something is good for you that even more of it is even better. NHS Choices warns that taking too much protein can have side effects, including diarrhoea. There is also evidence that, long-term, excessive protein intake may lead to an increased risk of osteoporosis leading to weak bones and risk of fracture. Instructions on packages should be clear about maximum daily amounts because of potential risks of harm. The Department of Health advises adults to avoid consuming more than twice the recommended daily intake of protein.

VITAMINS

Taking extra vitamins is also at best a waste of time if there is a normal diet and no underlying disease. Most of the water soluble vitamins such as vitamin C and the B complex are rapidly excreted in the urine if taken to excess. People who take "megadoses" of vitamin C every day may as well bypass the kidneys and put the tablets straight down the toilet. The fat soluble vitamins A, D and E if taken to excess can cause toxicity and disease. It is amazing how many people think that vitamin C is of value in the common cold. There is a mountain of evidence to show that it is totally useless yet many products for colds advertise that they "contain vitamin C". They do not actually say that it helps the cold but the consumer may well think so.

If you go to any so-called health food shop they will offer you a variety of vitamins and minerals for children, for the elderly, for middle aged people, for pregnant women, for athletes in training, for Uncle Tom Cobley and all. Some people may even try to tell you that these are a better way of treating disease as drugs are made by the pharmaceutical industry whose only interested is profits. Ask who makes the vitamin and mineral capsules. It is the same much maligned pharmaceutical industry. They may also offer you ginseng or other herbal concoctions with various spurious claims. Almost all of these have not been subjected to scientific scrutiny to see if they are effective or if they do any harm. It is naïve to believe that the absence of evidence is an index of safety. They may say that they have been extensively used or have been used for centuries. In the past we have used arsenic and lead in face creams and mercury to treat disease. Look at the substances taken in marathons in the early 20th century. For many centuries almost every disease was treated with bloodletting. These herbal remedies may be no more effective and no safer than these discredited treatments.

Beware the peddlers of alternative health. Beware the nutritionists. Some are good and scientifically trained. Some have spurious qualifications or none at all. It can be difficult to tell which is which. Just because a person assumes the title of doctor does not mean that they have a medical qualification or even a doctorate in an unrelated subject.

DIET

A glance at the names of the major sponsors of the Olympic Games and many other sporting events shows that the majority are purveyors of fast food and fizzy drinks. The two largest sponsors of the Olympics are Coca Cola and McDonalds. At the time when the London Olympics was *inspiring a generation* the Olympic Stadium boasted the largest McDonalds in the world. When fast food and sugary drinks are so often named as major culprits in the obesity epidemic we may ask why they are so eager to be associated with sport.

One suggestion is the inference that running around and doing some exercise will negate the adverse effects of these products. It is not their fault that we have so much obesity, even in children, but the lack of exercise. They are eager to promote exercise in schools and at the same time to promote themselves. There is a "halo effect" from promoting sport.

Tobacco companies also used to advertise in sport until this was banned in 2003 although for Formula One racing this was delayed until

2005. Bernie Ecclestone donated £1million to the Labour Party but he denied that this was linked to the delay in the advertising ban.

We are not happy about being overweight or obese and at any time many of us are on a diet. Perusal of any bookshop or library will show a wealth of books all claiming that their diet will give certain success. The fact that there are so many books promoting so many diets shows two facts. One is that there is an enormous market for diets. The other is that none is satisfactory or it would have cornered the market. These books are usually very short on science although they may boast some pseudoscience. Their biggest selling power comes from celebrity endorsement which is totally meaningless and valueless. Celebrities are not famous for their knowledge of science. Indeed, many are remarkably poorly informed about anything. Some just seem to be famous for being famous.

Probably all of the diets may be of some value in some circumstances. Sticking to a diet can be very difficult but if the dieter strays it is his or her fault and no fault of the diet. For those who do achieve their target weight many will bounce back again when they stop. About five years down the line only about six percent of people have kept the weight off. However, from a business perspective, having 94% of customers returning again and again is a dream come true.

Managing overweight and obesity is not simply a matter of getting down to the target weight. It requires a lifelong change in attitude and lifestyle. Organisations such as Weight Watchers do not promote a specific diet but offer support and advice in a more general way. Short term they are helpful but five years later any benefit has usually been lost.

There are products for sale that are supposed to replace a meal. There are far more that claim to be low in Calories. Too often the supposedly healthy options are nothing like as healthy as they pretend. Low Calorie soups are much reduced in fat but fat gives it much of its taste. There are two problems with this product. One is that it is less satisfying to the appetite and so the dieter is tempted to have a second helping or to eat something else. The other is that fat is replaced with salt and some low Calorie foods can be very high in salt. Salt has no Calories but it leads to high blood pressure. High blood pressure increases the risk of heart attacks and to an even greater extent strokes.

Foods may be promoted as healthy options but more often the claim is implicit rather than overt. They seem to have the right things such as fruit or fibre but overall they may be far from healthy. An Innocent Smoothy may be fruit based but it has more sugar than Coca Cola. Breakfast cereals with fruit, nuts and honey have more sugar and fat than standard cereals such as Weetabix. Porridge with added fruit and currants may sound even healthier than normal porridge until we find that about a quarter of it is sugar. Bread can be remarkably high in salt. For most of us careful examination of the label when out shopping is too difficult and time-consuming. The small print becomes impossible to read at the age when either reading glasses or longer arms are required. Therefore governments and chief medical officers have been keen to introduce a simple "traffic light" scheme but this has been successfully blocked by the food industry.

For those of us who like to keep fit and well, eating a healthy diet is essential regardless of any desire or need for weight loss. In the aftermath of the BSE outbreak and Salmonella in eggs many people flocked to the newly promoted fad of organic food. They shun insecticides, weed killers and chemical fertilisers, although what is and what is not allowed in organic farming is not as simple as may be thought. It is not really true to say that they ban chemical fertilisers. It is just that the chemicals come from manure rather than a purer form. This increases the risk of contamination of rivers with faecal material. It is not true to say that they ban insecticides either. They just limit them to certain "natural" products as if everything that is found in nature is completely safe. At the same time, genetically modified (GM) crops have been hysterically called "Frankenstein foods" and Europe has maintained a constant irrational opposition to them. They have been used extensively in North and South America as well as elsewhere in the world. There have never been any dangers to the public from GM foods. All new foods have to be rigorously tested before going on the market. On the other hand, organic food has resulted in many cases of food poisoning from E coli. This is a serious illness that often requires admission to hospital and it causes deaths. There is no evidence that organic food is any healthier but it is invariably more expensive.

A GM product called Golden Rice has been developed which contains beta carotene and so prevents vitamin A deficiency. However, Greenpeace have successfully prevented its release to developing countries that need it. Greenpeace can claim responsibility for the thousands of children who go blind every year from vitamin A deficiency because of their rigid and unquestioning dogmatism.

As mentioned earlier, alcohol gives 700 Calories per 100 grams and so reducing or eliminating it from the diet may help weight loss. The Calories removed are unlikely to be replaced by eating more. Indeed, alcohol can lower blood glucose and this may increase hunger. This is probably the rationale behind a dry sherry as an aperitif.

EXERCISE

The diet industry is massive and it is so commercially successful because of its low effectiveness. It offers us hope but long term it fails to deliver. Still we keep returning. The first law of thermodynamics states that energy can neither be created nor destroyed. This is the basis of the simple equation that if Calories taken in exceed Calories expended we gain weight. If Calories in are less than Calories out we lose weight and to maintain our weight we need an equilibrium between energy in and energy out. This leads on logically to the association between exercise and weight loss. It makes sense to try to mix diet and exercise in the pursuit of the ideal weight.

What we want to lose is fat. Each 100 grams of fat contains 930 Calories. Therefore we have to do 9,300 Calories of exercise to burn a kilogram of fat. This is roughly 3,500 Calories a pound for those who still use shillings and pence. If we go to the gym and do a 700 Calories workout, which many will find quite strenuous, even after 13 visits we have not yet burned a kilogram of fat. For the average person who is not very fit this may take 20 or more visits. In addition, the exertions of the gym may leave us doing less activity for the rest of the day and it may stimulate our appetite. As a nation we spend a great deal of money on gym memberships and many of those memberships are taken out with a view to losing weight. There is disillusionment when the weight does not fall away but contracts for gym membership is often for at least a year.

If the aim is simply to lose weight it probably represents a poor investment. It would be wrong to think that exercise has no part to play in losing weight. It may just be less than we think. There are many other benefits from physical activity. It reduces our risk of heart disease and diabetes. It may have some benefit on mental health, reducing depression and the risk of dementia. Exercise is to be commended in its own right. It may also help with weight in terms of creating a new self-image and a change in lifestyle. It may help to tone up muscle so that the flabby belly is less marked. We should be taking up exercise but we need to know why.

It may be wrong simply to count the Calories in and Calories out when assessing exercise and weight loss. When we go on a diet our body tends to switch to "famine mode" and becomes more economical in its use of food. In centuries and millennia past this would have been a great survival advantage as the danger to life was famine, not excess. It has been suggested that this accounts for some of the racial differences in the incidence of diabetes. People of African descent are about twice as susceptible to diabetes as those of European origin. Those of Indian ancestry are about six times as likely to suffer from diabetes. Some people hope that exercise will stop the body from adopting "famine mode" but I am yet to see good scientific evidence of this. It is also said that after brisk exercise the resting metabolic rate rises for up to 24 hours. However, this was based on some poor quality research in the first half of the 20th century and it has not been possible to reproduce it.

Exercise increases insulin sensitivity. This is good as insulin resistance is associated with type two diabetes, heart disease and strokes. Insulin also tends to stop the breakdown of fat, so reducing insulin levels with exercise may help to burn fat. A large amount of body fat increases the risk of type two diabetes. The risk is also increased by lack of exercise, a family history of type two diabetes and smoking.

If we reject dieting as a short term fix at best and exercise per se is of limited value in weight loss, what should we do? Weight is not gained suddenly. An obese person does not wake up one morning and say, "Look at the state of me. I was quite skinny when I went to bed last night." Before weight becomes troublesome we need to take it in hand. Keep it in check with regular weighing. The best plan is to get up in the morning, go to the toilet then stand on the scales naked. This is the lightest and most flattering weight of the day but also the most consistent. Do not worry if the scales are a little inaccurate as they will still show movements up or down. Do not be unduly concerned with charts. Look at yourself in a full length mirror and ask how it seems. People who have been greatly overweight are unlikely ever to achieve an "ideal" weight. A muscular person may have a body weight above that recommended and weight gain in pregnancy is normal. In pregnancy avoid eating for two.

For people who have been greatly overweight and many others we must accept that it is a life-long problem that requires long term attention. Avoid "yo-yo dieting". We are allowed to be "bad" once in a while as long as it does not become a habit. Be wary of what is promoted as healthy food. Traffic light schemes may be helpful but the food industry has opposed them. Read the packet carefully but do not become a slave to Calorie counting or become too obsessed by fat or other components of the diet. Eat a varied diet and try to get a range of colours in it. This will give a variety of vitamins and minerals and supplements of these are unnecessary.

Exercise is good and to be highly commended. It must be something that we enjoy or we shall not persevere. It has many health benefits and it does has a place is weight loss and a healthier lifestyle but the effect of Calories burned may be disappointing. A sedentary person probably requires about 1,800 Calories a day. An active person, perhaps with a physical job requires at least twice that. An excess of 50 Calories a day of energy in versus energy used results in nearly 2kg of fat every year, so watch it.

CONCLUSION

All that glistens is not gold. Much that is sold as supposedly having a scientific basis has none at all and may even be harmful. The NHS Choices website heads the article on body building with "Getting ripped or getting ripped off?" At present, provided that a product does not claim to cure a specific disease which would make it liable to control as a medicine, almost any fanciful claim can be made for supplements, drinks or "complementary and alternative medicines" without any evidence to back it up.

Sports drinks offer no advantage over water for the ordinary athlete. If we eat a normal diet we do not need supplements of protein or vitamins even if we are in training. We need to take weight in order before it becomes a serious problem. Exercise is highly beneficial but we need to do a lot of exercise to lose a little weight and it may make us hungrier.

We need either better consumer protection or a better educated public. The food industry has managed to block legislation that would make its labelling more transparent. There are sources of sound advice but few people know how to distinguish them from the snake oil salesmen.

It is not only sportsmen who bend the rules.

9. Picking up the Pieces

Y ou may now be totally disenchanted. Your favourite sport is riddled with bad sportsmanship if not overt cheating. Drug use is endemic and officials are corrupt. If you go jogging or go to the gym there are people eager to take advantage of you and to sell you products of dubious worth. Remember that this short book is about cheating in sport. Whilst it is far from comprehensive, a book about the glories of sport would have to be very much larger. The situation is merely a reflection of human nature. Most of us are good most of the time. There will always be people with a psychopathic personality who believe only in the 11th commandment: "Thou shalt not get caught". The situation is not beyond redemption but we must remember that a world of sport with no cheating is as unachievable as a society totally free of crime. That is not a reason to give up trying. Let us have a look at the issues and see what may be done.

SEX

To turn first to sex, I could find just one example of an overt man masquerading as a woman to compete. Nevertheless, gender issues in women's sport are important. Women are much more susceptible to being dominated by a large and powerful opponent than are men. No large and muscular man has dominated men's tennis in the way that the Williams sisters have dominated women's tennis for many years although the New Zealand rugby player Jonah Lomu at 196 centimetres and 120kg usually needed two opposing players to bring him down. In the 1990s the powerful Chinese women swimmers took the swimming medals despite poor style whilst the men were unimpressive. Although there is a difference between natural physique and the effect of anabolic steroids, the point is that women's sport needs a level playing field even more than men's. The abolition of mandatory gender testing is to be applauded and selective testing is much better. However, it seems that too much emphasis is placed on chromosomes and not enough on hormones. If a genetic abnormality can lead to a ban from women's events why should an endocrine (hormonal) problem be different? Both are diseases. The results of medical investigations are not made public in the name of medical confidentiality. On the one hand this is everyone's basic right and should be respected. On the other hand the absence of facts leads to speculation. Men who have had sex change operations, referred to by the politically correct as gender reassignment surgery, are allowed to compete as women after two years. This may be rather lenient after many years of exposure to male hormones. However, no transsexual seems to have made much of an impression on women's sport.

WHY CHEAT?

Sometimes we may wonder at the motivation for cheating. Is there pride in having a medal for finishing a marathon after missing out a large chunk of the course? The microchips in shoes should overcome this problem but it is sad that they are necessary. Sometimes cheating may be tempting because there is money at stake or in the case of the Xiamen marathon in China, extra points towards university entrance. We may seek to blame the vast amount of money to be earned from sport and it certainly plays a part but cheating occurs even in amateur sport. Where is the glory in an ill-won victory? Perhaps it is the issue of "famous for 15 minutes". Imagine a CV saying, "I won a gold medal in the Paralympics as a mentally handicapped player but I am not really mentally deficient." There was the criminal assault of getting a "hit-man" to try to disable an opponent. This was in amateur ice skating although the status of amateur may be an illusion. Perhaps there is a psychopathic attitude that cheating is only ignominious if you get caught. We must remember that cheating is not limited to drug abuse and the authorities must be vigilant.

Sometimes cheating, such as drug use, is ubiquitous and the mantra is "Be a user or a loser". This can also lead to the feeling from athletes that it is not immoral to cheat if everyone else is doing the same. This was Ben Johnson's stance. Lance Armstrong also told the BBC that he felt that he had been treated harshly. He was in a sport that was rampant with drug abuse. Somehow we must get the mentality embedded that because others are cheating that does not justify it. If one individual of many is singled out he will naturally feel aggrieved. It is very difficult for the athlete who does not win and he thinks that it is because all who do better are cheats. This applies to far more than just drug use. Much of the pressure must come from the fans and they must also set an example as exemplary fans. They must not try to intimidate referees into making bad decisions. They must give due credit to opponents who perform well. They must not overlook foul play just because it comes from the team that they support.

SPORTSMANSHIP AND SPORT

If an action is not actually illegal that does not make it acceptable. In the 2012 Olympics some badminton players tried to lose and there was the 800 metres runner who dropped out and then gave a spurious medical certificate. The authorities were able to take action and in some cases they did but they could have done more. It is important for the people who pay for sport, namely the fans and the sponsors, to make it clear that they regard such antics as unacceptable. For both fans and sponsors it seems that too often the end justifies the means and all that matters is a good result. Mind games are becoming commoner and are difficult to police. Probably the best defence comes from the advice of sports psychologists and understanding what is going on. Cricket, which we used to regard as quintessentially embodying sportsmanship, is becoming a very unpleasant game, especially against the Australians. However, the authorities in all sports should also make their displeasure clear and threaten sanctions. We want to see sportsmanship back in sport. A little discipline at the weigh-in before a boxing match would not go amiss.

KEEPING UP

We should question but not necessarily reject new and expensive technology. The British bobsleigh team uses technology developed for the Typhoon fighter plane. Swimming suits that cost hundreds of pounds and can be used only a few times have been discussed. The problems of prosthetics and other aids in disabled sport have been mentioned. We must not deny all improvements but we need to keep the cost of competing realistic. With regard to technology we must keep a balance between avoiding the Luddite tendency to reject any innovation and finding that competing in that sport is so expensive that it is open only to those with substantial financial backing. Is it a contest between sportsmen or a competition between scientists?

There is a constant battle between those who would use performance enhancing substances and the authorities that are responsible for catching them. Whenever an athlete is found to have tested positive for drugs there is always a hysterical outcry that someone could do such a thing. Instead we should congratulate the testers. This outcry is both naïve and hypocritical, especially when orchestrated by journalists whose own profession has fallen well short in terms of ethics and compliance with the law. There will always be a temptation to cheat and there will always be those who will succumb.

Although cheating occurred well before sport became a major money earner and it persists even in amateur events it would be naïve to suggest that finance plays no part in the temptation. In English football the difference that it makes to a club to be promoted or relegated between the premiership and the championship or to play champions' league football comes to millions of pounds per season. There is also the money that rests on gambling. Top athletes need sponsorship and the sponsors like their prodigies to be constantly amongst the elite. Just doing well once every four years at the Olympics or even annually at world championships is not enough. If they slip down the rankings they may see a reduction in their sponsorship or even have it removed. Not only does this affect their salary but they may have to face clawing their way back up through the rankings with less financial support to buy themselves the best facilities. If they lose their salary they may have to hold a job while they train. As athletes get older it becomes more difficult, especially recovery from injury and the temptation to turn to drugs is great.

Money does play a great part in elite sport and with such enormous earnings at stake it is hard to criticise those who follow the gold. It is also very difficult to see how the spiralling amount of money paid to players can be curtailed. It is easy to see how it is possible to buy success in English Premiership football. The enormous injection of capital into Chelsea and Manchester City are not the only examples. It was ironic that Sir Alex Ferguson criticised this change when he used to manage the only club in the top division who had much more money than the rest. Around Christmas when players were getting tired and injuries were becoming a problem other managers would have to suffice with a pep talk to the team whilst he could go out and buy a few more world class players. The Indian Premier Cricket League has created levels of pay that other games of cricket are unable to match. The problem is not limited to the heavily endowed team sports. Some Kenyan runners have accepted offers to become nationals of Gulf States in return for far more money than they could possibly earn in their own country. We do need to ask if this is just economic reality that must be accepted or if the rules should be changed. We have seen that changing allegiance to another city state occurred back in the Ancient Olympics. In the early days of the modern Olympics it was just the rich who could afford the time to train and the money to travel to events. Now there may be sponsorship and greater opportunities but money still rules.

DRUGS

Of the 5,000 or more drug tests that were performed at the London Olympics, just 13 were positive. Nevertheless attention is focussed on the 13 positive tests rather than the 4,987 or more negative ones. This small number of positive tests may mean that rigorous testing has discouraged those who would use drugs or it may mean that more sophisticated ways have been devised to avoid detection. Both are probably true but in some countries it would seem that the latter is the principle reason for negative tests. More than 100 athletes who may have competed were barred because they had received a ban for positive tests. On the one hand we should not focus on the few who test positive for drugs but celebrate the many who compete without such advantages. On the other hand, we have reason to believe that most drug users never get caught, especially when they have sophisticated scientific backing. The World Anti-doping Agency (WADA) was formed in November 1999 and is constantly trying to learn about new techniques in performance enhancement and how to detect them. For every scientist in the world who works at improving detection there are probably 50 to 100 who work at avoiding detection. The athletes may feel under considerable pressure and in some countries they simply have to do what they are told. There is still state sponsored doping with the scientific resources of the state behind it. However, the fact that some people are being weeded out means that drugs cannot be used with total impunity.

The 1980 Olympics in Moscow had no positive drug test reported and after it Prince Alexandre de Mérode, the current head of the IOC medical commission described the games as "the purest ever". This was either blatant sarcasm or grossly naïve as at the time drug taking was rife and drug testing was in its infancy. He was not a doctor or a chemist but a Belgian nobleman and a historian. He was also a chain smoker who died of lung cancer.

There have been a number of important landmarks in the history of doping where systems could have been improved but the chance was passed by. After the Ben Johnson affair in 1998 the Canadian government set up a commission called the Dubin Inquiry. It started in February 1989 and sat for 11 months. It was chaired by Charles Dubin who was Chief Justice for Ontario and lead counsel was Bob Armstrong. Both were very experienced lawyers and very keen sports fans. The atmosphere of the inquiry was fairly relaxed and not too inquisitorial. As a result they probably obtained far more honesty than an aggressive stance would have achieved. Journalists and politicians love a "full public inquiry" but in reality a confidential inquiry gives much better results. Any witness would be much more willing to be candid to a confidential inquiry than to a public inquiry where perceived shortcomings will lead to public ridicule. Non-threatening confidential inquiries are not a cover up but the best way to the truth and learning lessons from past mistakes. Journalists dislike confidential inquiries because they deny them a circus. The Dubin Inquiry found that the use of drugs in top level sport was almost ubiquitous. Some may criticise the inquiry for being too focussed on Canada but there is no reason to believe that what was happening there was not also happening in the rest of the world. They recommended out of season testing for steroids and the International Olympic Committee (IOC) duly ignored them. Overcoming inertia seems to be very difficult for the IOC. Their history is littered with turning a blind eye to doping and even ignoring or losing positive results.

Testing athletes for banned substances at events is not enough and out of season testing has eventually been introduced. Representatives of the governing bodies may arrive unannounced and demand a drug test. Failure to comply is seen as an admission of guilt. The trouble is that this is not policed on an international basis but by the national governing bodies. This accounts for the absence of positive tests from countries such as China, Cuba and North Korea. It is also very difficult to get to athletes from Kenya and Ethiopia. The drug testing system in Jamaica is not up to standard. The trouble is that national bodies are being asked to weed out and disqualify their own sporting heroes.

When Ben Johnson tested positive for stanazolol in 1988 a doctor from the laboratory tested both that sample and one he had from Rome the previous year and he said that the testosterone levels were fluctuating. Women have a significant change of hormone levels through the menstrual cycle although this is rather less with oral contraceptives. Men have a rather more steady level, although, as we have seen, that level can vary significantly between individuals. Taking other androgens including synthetic hormones will suppress testosterone levels by suppressing the driving hormones from the pituitary gland. Taking testosterone would raise them. Significant fluctuations of testosterone levels out of season may indicate steroid use but this is a personal suggestion and it would have to be validated.

Some people claim that erythropoietin (EPO) should be legal as it is safe but others suggest that perhaps 20 European cyclists died as a result of EPO use in the early 1990s. Altitude training is also potentially dangerous but it is legal. Mountain sickness from too rapid ascent can be fatal. Banning altitude training is not a viable option.

It is extremely naïve to believe that herbs can have all the benefits of drugs without any of the adverse effects. Some may have been adulterated with anabolic steroids or other substances including stimulants. Competitors would do well to stay away from all such things. Even if they are not adulterated, they have not been adequately researched and they may well do more harm than good. Oriental preparations such as ginseng are very popular in this field and adulterated Chinese products are well described. One that was reported in the medical press was a Chinese herbal cream for eczema in infants. It was found to contain betamethasone (Betnovate™) which is a strong steroid cream that should not be used by babies. Nor should it be used on the face by anyone. This cream would have been applied to the face of babies.

We need to get rid of the idea from athletes, coaches and society as a whole that there is something almost magical about herbs, especially oriental herbs. They are not effective but safe drugs that scientific medicine has meticulously avoided. They are not ignored by scientists and the pharmaceutical industry because it is impossible to patent a natural substance and hence to make money from it. The production process can be patented or the molecule can be refined and patented. There are many drugs that originate from herbs or natural organisms including digoxin, penicillin, quinine, aspirin and morphine. The problem is that anything that is classified as a medicine faces restrictions whilst herbal concoctions have often never been tested for efficacy or safety and it is foolish to assume both. This is before they get adulterated with pharmaceutical products.

Richard Moore in his book "*The dirtiest race in history*" quotes Ben Johnson more than 20 years later as saying that natural vitamins have been improved so much that they have the same effect as performance enhancing drugs. However, he believes that there is still a great deal of drug use. The idea that purer vitamins enhance performance is naïve. It does not matter whether an athlete takes 100% pure vitamin supplements or good old-fashioned fruit and vegetables, his body will get the vitamins and minerals it needs. Because something is good for you, such as vitamins, does not mean that even more and ever purer is even better. However, it might be in the mind and the placebo effect must not be underestimated. If the athlete believes that something will improve his performance it will. Another possibility is that Ben Johnson is being naïve and what he is told is purely a vitamin or mineral supplement really contains performance enhancing drugs. This was certainly the case in East Europe and may still be true in China and elsewhere.

It is tempting to suggest that the battle against doping is lost as so much is obviously still occurring and so we should give up. To do so would be as illogical as to say that because we still have crime the police force has failed and it should be disbanded. We should instead be increasing the resources of the testers. This includes an international approach to out of season testing. Do negative tests mean a cleaner sport or smarter cheaters? To suggest that five percent of those who take drugs get caught is probably over optimistic but it is impossible to get true figures. Lance Armstrong had more than 600 negative tests. The imposition of life long bans for anyone who tests positive will not reduce the incidence of cheating any more than longer prison sentences reduce crime. Abolition of the death penalty for murder did not result in an upsurge in murders and in countries where drug trafficking carries the death penalty people still do it. Tougher sentences are not a deterrent if people do not expect to get caught. If the chance of getting caught was to increase substantially that would be a very different matter. An automatic life ban for offenders would be applauded by some but there are people who maintain steadfastly that they did not knowingly take a banned substance. Perhaps a member of the coaching team or an outsider had administered it without their knowledge. One who persistently denied wrongdoing was Maria Koch and she never had a positive test, but her letter to the authorities complaining of not getting as much steroid as her teammate came to light. We may be cynical but there may be some genuine people. It is possible to prove that a person has taken drugs. It is not possible to prove that an individual has never taken them. Some offenders re-offend, as with crime, but assuming that they will all reoffend is inappropriate, especially if the difference between one with a conviction and one without is simply that the one with the conviction got caught. This is true of both crime and drugs use in sport as only a minority get caught. If they have done their crime and done their time they should be rehabilitated, even if watched more closely than others. Dwayne Chambers admitted his guilt and has since been vocal in telling others not to do the same. He should be welcomed back as a penitent man. Just as it is too often the small time criminals who get caught whilst organised crime remains relatively immune, so too it is the amateurish bumbling offender who tests positive and not those who have a nation's resources behind them for effective doping and avoidance. The problem is what goes on behind closed doors in closed countries. Sport is war without the bloodshed and nations will seek to win glory from sport as much as they do in battle. To the victor go the spoils.

We now have abundant documentary evidence of the level of drug use in the old East Germany and it has been suggested that all those athletes should be stripped of their Olympic medals and world records and that these should be handed to those who came up behind them. Tempting as the proposal may seem it has the major problem that it assumes that those who came along behind were clean. We know very well that drug abuse was not limited to East Germany or the Soviet Bloc but it was very extensive in the West too. Hence such action may simply take the accolades from one group of cheats and give it to another. This is the problem with historical cases. Of course when an athlete tests positive immediately after an event any medal or record from that event does not stand. There is also a problem that if one member of a relay teams test positive then all the team lose their medal or record although only the offender is disciplined. Punishing all for the sins of one may seem unfair. However, if one member of the team makes a bad hand-over or a false start the whole team is disqualified and this is no different. It may also put more pressure on the drug users not to let down the team.

Perhaps coaches and other members of the coaching team at top level should be licensed. This may help to get rid of some of the "snake-oil salesmen" but it also means that anyone who is implicated in cheating in any form may lose his licence.

Getting drugs out of sport is an impossible task but there are many steps that can be taken to make it more difficult. The trouble is that out of season testing requires the compliance of the countries whose athletes will be exposed. It is much easier to make the right noises but to do nothing.

It would also be useful to make it clear that taking herbal supplements and hence inadvertently taking a banned drug is not an acceptable excuse. These herbal substances are often taken in the belief that they have performance enhancing effects whilst not being illegal. If this is true then the intent is to use a performance enhancing substance. No one knows if these substances are beneficial or not as proper scientific trials have never been done. In reality they are probably useless unless they have been adulterated with pharmacological agents as happens all too often. This is true of a great deal of the dogma that surrounds training and performance. One famous dictum is that athletes should abstain from sexual intercourse before an event. I have found only two papers on the subject in reputable scientific journals. One found no adverse effect and the other found none unless intercourse occurred within two hours of the event. That is barely enough time to get the shorts back on.

We saw that BALCO charged a great deal of money to provide what was ostensibly a scientific training regime or at least a drug taking regime. The drugs included anabolic steroids and EPO that are known to enhance performance but the rest of the scientific regime was probably a mirage. It is very difficult to conduct trials of an adequate size for the effects of illegal drugs. A survey of the scientific literature will not show such trials as they would not have had the approval of ethics committees. However, countries in which there is large scale state sponsored drug taking may be able to do so.

CORRUPTION

Corruption of officials must be addressed. Too often sporting bodies have ignored the problem. It is easy to pretend that it does not exist. That applies to both the IOC and FIFA, the world football authority. Under Jacques Rogge the IOC may have started to take it seriously but FIFA still has much to prove. Officials who take bribes must not only be thrown out of their organisation but they should face criminal charges too. The ethos must be one of proud independence, not boasting that things can be achieved if the price is right.

It would be wrong to dismiss Jacques Rogge as another failure because some of his officials have been caught misbehaving on his watch. What matters is how he responded to it. There are still many who would dismiss him as just another impotent figure on the gravy train of world sport. This would seem unfair. He has not managed to clean up the sport and officials completely but he has made some notable advances. There are far too many countries in which corruption is still endemic and bribing officials is accepted as the standard way to get things done. We may be impressed by the achievements of the soaring economies of the BRIC countries and other developing nations but we may wonder more what they would have achieved if their economies were not stagnated by widespread corruption. It is a blight that keeps much of the world in poverty. It is very tempting to ignore an embarrassing problem such as corruption or drug taking but that does not make it go away. It must be confronted and addressed.

Jacques Rogge has now been succeeded at the IOC by the German Thomas Bach. He is an outspoken critic of doping. He commissioned an academic report, published in July 2013, which alleged that West German as well as East German athletes had been involved in malpractice during the Cold War and before the unification of the two countries. However, his first challenge as head of the IOC was the 2014 Winter Games as the Russians have taken an aggressive anti-homosexual stand.

Judges and referees also need to be seen to be fiercely independent. As with higher officials, actual corruption of judges must be taken very seriously. Sometimes it is very difficult not to be intimidated by a highly partisan home crowd. Crowds who would intimidate a judge or an opponent to give advantage to their side are like athletes who would cheat to win and just as despicable. As a fan do you go to see a good sporting contest or do you go solely to see your team win by fair means or foul? Excessive national pride or incompetence in referees is not uncommon. However, in fairness to referees, they have to make an instant decision on the spot. We can all criticise referees when we watch "*Match of the Day*" with slow motion replay from three different angles but they do not have this advantage. On first sight without action replays, I must admit that referees get it right much more often than I do. Wherever feasible, in big important events they should have the backup of technology. We have this this in cricket, tennis and rugby and at last it has been admitted to Premier League football although FIFA has opposed its introduction to international matches.

SPORTS PRODUCTS

Making sure that we do not get ripped off by false claims when we participate in sport is no easy task. We may believe that under the Trades Descriptions Act that what it says on the bottle it must do. The problem is a mixture of ambiguity and implied rather than overt claims as well as some lethargy in prosecuting offenders. There is also the problem of interpreting the evidence, if we know it. A product may offer some benefit to trained athletes in the abnormal condition of training after eating and drinking nothing since the previous day. That does not necessarily mean that if we go training after breakfast that we shall also benefit.

The sports drinks and nutrition industries offer a great deal of money to sport and both the sporting bodies and the Government are reluctant to do anything that may impair this flow. However, we do need to see some honesty. Drug companies may fund research on their own products but they do not normally have members on committees such as NICE that decide if their products should be recommended. This is not the case with sports drinks and many who give expert advice are in their pay.

It is very easy to be taken in by the supposedly expert advice about sports drinks but there are other ways in which a little common sense along with just a little knowledge and an enquiring mind can help. Does it really make sense that sweating more without doing any more exercise helps to burn fat? If it did we could sit in a sauna doing nothing whilst the fat melts away. Does any lethargic teenager believe that he is full of energy and vitality because he walks around with a bottle of drink containing sugar and caffeine? Perhaps he is addicted to the caffeine and needs to break this dependence. Why buy expensive protein supplements instead of ordinary food? Is our normal diet really deficient in protein or vitamins? People are not taught how to question and how to think.

One of the problems about health, sport and nutrition is the plethora of people who call themselves nutritionists despite an absence of appropriate qualifications. They often claim to be at the cutting edge of research in the subject but they do not have a single paper published in a reputable scientific journal. In his book *"Bad Science"* Ben Goldacre points out that terms such as nutritionist, nutritional therapist and nutritional consultant can be used by anyone. Claims to be a dietician, physiotherapist or nurse require appropriate qualifications. Titles such as doctor or professor can also be claimed with impunity. He devotes a whole chapter to someone who styles herself as Dr Gillian McKeith PhD. She is not a medical doctor but has a PhD from Clayton College of Natural Health in Birmingham Alabama. Normally a PhD requires a thesis based on at least three years of personal research but from this school the only qualification required was a valid credit card. The school closed in 2010 largely in the face of law suits from former students who were fundamentally accusing it of fraud.

Ben Goldacre also devoted a whole chapter to Professor Patrick Holford. He was awarded a lower second class degree in Psychology by the University of York after which he worked as a salesman of supplement pills. A year later he started treating patients. He started an MPhil degree in nutrition at the University of Surrey but he never finished it. In 1995 he was awarded a diploma by the Institute of Optimal Nutrition, a body which he set up in 1984 and he was director until 1998. Despite his lack of qualifications or publications in respected scientific journals he was appointed visiting professor at Teesside University, almost certainly because they thought that he could bring money to the department. He resigned in 2008 amidst a great outcry about his appointment but Mr Holford still assumes the title of professor. He accuses anyone who challenges him of being in the pay of big pharmaceutical firms but he is the one who has made a great deal of money from selling vitamin pills. He has also published many books which make such claims as vitamin C is more useful than antiretroviral therapy in the treatment of AIDS. I found six of his books in my local library. It has quite an extensive section on medical and related matters but about three quarters of these books should really be in the fiction section under science fiction or fantasy.

Quacks and charlatans are often invited to expound their views on television by totally uncritical presenters and they may come over as plausible. The presenters usually have a degree in the humanities and no understanding of science. Website such as Quack Watch (www.quackwatch.com) and Sense About Science (www.senseaboutscience.org) are worth a visit as well as an entire website devoted to Holford Watch. There are people who try to bring the public the truth but they are fighting a losing battle in the face of widespread public ignorance. As a nation we spend millions of pounds each year on so called complementary and alternative medicine that is of no value and millions more on vitamin pills and supplements. People will believe what they want to believe. They seem quite determined to be taken in. They want a quick fix.

The series of articles in the *BMJ* about the bad science and problems of sports drinks was not picked up by the general press who tend to watch the *BMJ* and *Lancet* for possible sensation. At least I never saw anything in any national newspaper. On the other hand a brief case study that was not even research, suggesting a possible link between the MMR vaccine and autism was widely reported but not the very many subsequent papers that refuted the claim. It even transpired that the original case report was fraudulent but a great deal of damage was done to children's health.

The food and drink industry appear to be intent on profit without any regard for social responsibility. They have successfully opposed the traffic lights scheme for food. They continue to market foods as healthy when they are not. They have often been compared to the tobacco industry which set about trying to discredit the enormous amount of evidence about the dangers of its product. More than 50 years since the Royal College of Physicians published "*Smoking and Health*" and its contents became widely known, people still take up smoking. The tobacco industry says that it does not aim to recruit young people but the age group with the highest rate of smoking is 15 to 24 years old.

We need a mixture of a better educated public and much more draconian legislation. The main impediment to legislation is that politicians have to see it as a public demand that will earn them political capital. Too many people do not even realise what is happening. Politicians will not take up a cause if they do not think that it will give them credit.

There will always be cheats in sport. There will always be some officials and judges who lack integrity. There will always be those who misrepresent products they wish to sell and offer pseudoscience or some new age nonsense to the gullible. As the Irish writer and philosopher Edmund Burke wrote, "All that is necessary for the triumph of evil is that good men do nothing." The late 13th century, early 14th century writer Dante Alighieri wrote in his *Inferno* that, "The hottest places in hell are reserved for those who, in times of great moral crisis, maintain their neutrality." No single individual will succeed in changing the world but each and every one of us, as individuals must insist on greater integrity in sport, in marketing and in life. If we do not oppose cheating in all its forms, then silence implies consent.

ND - #0216 - 270225 - C0 - 234/156/7 - PB - 9781780914169 - Gloss Lamination